KAREN ZACARÍAS: PLAYS ONE

T0353273

Karen Zacarías

PLAYS ONE

The Book Club Play
Destiny of Desire
Native Gardens

methuen | drama

LONDON • NEW YORK • OXFORD • NEW DELHI • SYDNEY

METHUEN DRAMA
Bloomsbury Publishing Plc
50 Bedford Square, London, WC1B 3DP, UK
1385 Broadway, New York, NY 10018, USA
29 Earlsfort Terrace, Dublin 2, Ireland

BLOOMSBURY, METHUEN DRAMA and the Methuen Drama logo
are trademarks of Bloomsbury Publishing Plc

First published in Great Britain by Oberon Books 2019

This edition published by Methuen Drama 2022

Cover image: (L to R) Steve Hendrickson as Frank Butley, Sally Wingert as Virginia
Butley, Jacqueline Correa as Tania Del Valle, and Dan Domingues as Pablo Del Valle
in Native Gardens, which was performed from September 15-October 22, 2017 at
Arena Stage at the Mead Center for American Theater. Photo by Dan Norman for
Guthrie Theater.

A catalogue record for this book is available from the British Library.

A catalog record for this book is available from the Library of Congress.

ISBN: PB: 978-1-3503-7193-4
eBook: 978-1-7868-2632-9

Series: Modern Plays

To find out more about our authors and books visit www.bloomsbury.com
and sign up for our newsletters.

Contents

THE BOOK CLUB PLAY

The Book Club Play received its world premiere at
Round House Theatre, Blake Robison, artistic director,
January-February 2008. It was subsequently presented at
Berkshire Theatre Festival, Stockbridge, Mass.,
Kate Maguire, artistic director, July 13-20, 2008, and at
Arena Stage, Washington, D.C., Molly Smith, artistic
director, Oct. 9-Nov. 6, 2008.

Development of *The Book Club Play* was supported
by the Eugene O'Neill Theater Center during a residence at
the National Playwrights Conference of 2007
and at the Playwrights' Center in Minneapolis, Dr. Polly
Carl, producing artistic director.

Characters

ANA SMITH (w): 30s. Pronounced "Ah-nuh." Beautiful. Charming. Smart. Accomplished. Organized. A columnist for a daily paper. The "Mother Bee." Her grace masks a need to control.

ROBERT NOVUM SMITH JR (m): 30s. ANA's golden-boy, handsome, charismatic, underachiever husband who is starting to search for meaning. Met in college. Upper-crust background.

WILLIAM LEE NOTHNAGEL (m): 30s. ROB's conservative, well-read, well-dressed, disciplined college roommate. ANA's former boyfriend. History buff. Unmarried.

JENNIFER McCLINTOCK (w): 30s. ANA's friend. Pretty. Shy. Smart. Tends to burst out with awkward truthful comments. Despite some lack of self-confidence, she is the grounding center of the group. Unorganized and oblivious to her own attractiveness. Unmarried.

LILY LOUISE JACKSON (w): Black, 20s. A go-getter. Former debate captain who is on the cusp of all current trends and yet can still put her foot in her mouth in social occasions. Laughs at appropriate and inappropriate times. A great lover of books and ANA's protégée at the paper.

ALEX (m): 30s. The new guy. A very smart, well-read academic who has lost his moorings and is searching for real connection. Professor of comparative literature.

PUNDIT (either): Plays five characters: SAM, Wal-Mart guy; FRANK, Secret Service agent; ELSA, jaded literary agent; MRS. SIMPSON, skydiver; CARL, inmate book dealer.

Character Notes

Pace and flow is vital for this play.

For professional productions: Double the roles, using only six actors. The PUNDITS can be played by the following characters with fast minimal costume changes (one or two articles at most):

> ELSA, jaded literary agent – played by JEN
> FRANK, Secret Service agent – played by WILL
> SAM, Wal-Mart guy – played by ROB
> CARL, inmate book dealer – played by ALEX
> MRS. SIMPSON, skydiver – played by LILY

If you are using a seventh actor for all the PUNDITS, then a fuller transformation can occur, so long as the pace and flow is unaffected. The seventh actor MUST play all the PUNDIT roles as written, man or woman.

For non-professional productions: The cast can be expanded to eleven actors by having each of the PUNDIT roles played individually.

Casting Note

ALEX can be cast in any race or ethnicity. LILY must be black. ANA, JEN, WILL and ROB can be any race or ethnicity except black.

Setting

A living room in the United States circa now.

Production Notes

This play is stylized like a film documentary. The characters know that they are being filmed but forget sometimes.

Names of the experts and titles of the books should be projected, but all the roles, including the PUNDITS, should be live. All the dialogue should be spoken by live actors, not filmed. The set-up is a film documentary, but the language is theatrical.

This is not a farce; it is a play about real people. The funny should come from the humanity of the characters.

Discussion and Engagement

The Book Club Play is as much about connection as it is about books. Theatre patrons could write their favorite book on an adhesive name tag as they walk into the theatre and wear it during the play to spark discussion during intermission. At the end of the performance, the stickers could be placed on a banner when they leave, so that people can see and discuss the books others have read. Book drives and video "confessionals" of reading pleasures to "Lars Knudsen" are all various easy ways to engage audiences in discussing books before and after the play.

Act I

Projection: **The Book Club: A Documentary.**

Spotlight: ANA SMITH **[name flashes on screen]**.

ANA: And my idea for Book Club was, simply, why don't I
start a club where we all read books… together! I came up
with it a good sixteen months before Oprah. Connection.
Bridges. Revelation… all of those were part of my impetus
to start the Book Club. Book Club is a safe haven… a
place to read, talk and to be our authentic selves *(Beat.)*
Was that OK? I'm happy to do it over again if you want it
better.

Spotlight: LILY LOUISE JACKSON **[name flashes on screen]**.

LILY: Why Book Club? Well, I like to read. I'm a writer…
although, right now I'm more of an editor and fact-finder
at the *Herald*. Ana, who's a columnist at the paper, invited
me to Book Club. To come every month and hang with
her and her old–not "old" old, but you know… longtime
mature-age type friends. I just moved here to start the job
and I don't know anyone, so I didn't really have a good
excuse for not coming. So, why not Book Club?

Spotlight: ROBERT NOVUM SMITH JR. **[name flashes on screen]**.

ROB: My wife, Ana, and my best friend, Will, started Book
Club way back. I don't think they even asked me to
join; it was kind of assumed I would be there. I'm not a
particular big reader. But I like being around great people.
I like being around good food. And it usually happens at
my house. So I'm already there. I guess Book Club just
sort of happened to me.

Spotlight: JENNIFER McCLINTOCK **[name flashes on screen]**.

JEN: Books are like best friends to me. Truth be told, I like books more than I like most people. I'm a paralegal at a law firm where I deal with the "fine print," and angry clients, and stressed out attorneys. Book Club is a place that reminds me of the better parts of being human. It is the only place in my life where the idea of community really thrives. I truly believe a good book and a good friend can bring out the best in a person. Even me.

*Spotlight: WILLIAM LEE NOTHNAGEL **[name flashes on screen]**.*

WILL: I simply adore books. I seriously considered getting a master's in library science, but the whole idea of letting other people take home books I had so carefully tended and organized, distressed me. Book Club is the best of two worlds. I share what I have read with people that I like, but then I take my own beautiful book home with me.

Projection: *Moby Dick* by Herman Melville.

ANA, ROB, WILL and LILY are all downstage looking at the audience.

ANA: *(Looking at her watch.)* OK. People. Places! Places! It's almost time. Five–four–three–two–Red light! It's on! It's on!

ROB: That's amazing!

ANA: *(Clears her throat, to the camera.)* Hello there. I am Ana Smith. Although you might recognize me… from my picture byline for my "Connections" column in the style section of the *Herald*, I am here in a very different role.

ROB: This is so weird.

WILL: Shhh.

ANA: And I am surrounded by some very special people, Rob, Lily, Will–say hello!

LILY & WILL: Hello.

ANA: Rob, honey—Say hello.

ROB: To who? Nobody's there.

ANA: Please say hello to the camera, dear.

ROB: Hello.

ANA: This wonderful man is my husband: Robert Novum Smith Jr.

And this is Lily. This amazing, hip young woman just moved from…

LILY: Akron, Ohio

ANA: Lily is an assistant editor at the *Herald*.

LILY: Thanks to Ana, I've also written some short opinion pieces for the metro section.

ANA: Oh Lily, I see a slightly younger me in you! It's so fun to hang outside of work.

LILY: It sure is, Ana.

WILL: Salutations.

ANA: This is William Lee Nothnagel the third. Our first member and our dearest friend.

WILL: I am curator of Greek antiquities at the History Museum.

ANA: And one of the best dressed and best read men that I know.

WILL: Brooks Brothers and a good book, what could be better?

ANA: *(Turns to the audience.)* This is most of my Book Club. TA-DA

JEN walks in late, harried, and still reading Moby Dick.

ANA: *(Cont'd, introduces her.)* Jennifer Mclintock… an old childhood friend of Will's and now a longtime cherished Book Club member.

JEN: Good God Jupiter, is that the… thingy?

LILY: It's moving.

ANA: It's focusing… It has a sensor that detects movement. *(Some of the Book Clubbers test it by moving.)* From seven p.m. to midnight its records everything from here to here.

JEN: Really?

ANA: Yes. Jen. 7p.m. Sharp.

LILY: Amazing.

ANA: This state of the art camera is transmitting images to… none other than the documentary director Lars Knudsen.

JEN: Lars Knudsen!?

WILL: I can't believe this! Lars Knudsen!

LILY: I loved his film *Hard Hats.*

WILL: Mesmerizing! It was all about construction workers in Canada.

ROB: Who is Lars–

ANA: KNUDSEN?

LILY: He is a cutting edge documentary director from Denmark whose work captures the essence of humanity by unobtrusively filming real people going about their real lives in real time.

ANA: And our Danish director is focusing on the American phenomenon of Book Clubs. And our Book Club is going to be the centerpiece of his study.

Book clubs are one of the biggest social groups in America … people want them… people need them. I know I do.

LILY: When you first brought it up, I thought it sounded like a hokey local cable access project. But, Ana, this is fantastic.

ROB: I've always secretly wanted to be on a reality show.

ANA: Rob. This is a serious documentary study by a renowned international director. Now as for the camera. *(Everyone looks at it.)* Look away! *(Everyone looks in different directions.)* Pretend it's not there. Act natural. Make yourselves comfortable. More comfortable. *(All pretending to be relaxed and comfortable… but not succeeding.)* It'd not be out of the realm of possibility that this could end up in Cannes.

WILL: Cannes! Fantastic!

JEN: *(Blurts.)* It's dreadful.

ANA: Excuse me?

JEN: *(Beat, touches her lips.)* I said that out loud, didn't I?

LILY & WILL: You did.

JEN: I'm really sorry. I didn't mean to…

WILL: Jenny, this is a great opportunity for our Book Club.

JEN: But why does our Book Club need an opportunity?

ANA: Because when a wonderful Book Club works so well for so long, it becomes our responsibility to share it with others.

JEN: But won't having THAT bug-eyed thing looking at us—change us?

ANA: Lars Knudsen is very clear—Nothing will change. We will take turns picking the books. All of us will read it and discuss. The big difference is we will meet here for filming every two weeks.

LILY: A new book every two weeks?!

ANA: Lars has some film festival deadlines; I thought we could handle the reading pressure.

WILL: Of course we can handle the reading! Right?

ALL: Right.

WILL: After all, Book Club is all about the books.

ROB: I thought Book Club was about the food.

ANA: Book Club is food for the mind and nourishment for the soul. And since I am the one that dragged us all into this crazy adventure, here at our house, I will be happy to cook all the meals

WILL: Glorious food by Ana.

LILY: But can we use your kitchen to cook when it's our book?

ANA: Use my kitchen?

JEN: Or just order take-out?

ANA: Take out? *(Beat.)* Of course! Whatever you need. Your book. Your meeting. It will just happen to be at our house.

LILY: With a freaky looking camera on us.

All laugh.

ANA: Rob, why don't you bring in the wine and lox dip I whipped up?

ROB: Great idea, Ana.

ANA: And let us begin with Will's book selection *Moby Dick; or, The Whale* by Herman Melville. A classic American novel.

WILL: "Call me Ishmael. Some years ago–never mind how long precisely–having little or no money in my purse, and nothing particular to interest me on shore, I thought I would sail about a little and see the watery part of the world. Whenever I find myself growing grim about the mouth; whenever it is a damp drizzly November in my soul; whenever it requires strong moral principle to prevent me from deliberately stepping into the street or knocking people's hats off, then I account it high time to get to the sea as soon as possible. This is my substitute for pistol and ball."

ANA: Sublime reading, Will.

WILL: Thank you, Ana.

ROB: Great job, buddy.

LILY: A classic in every sense of the word. Right, Jen?

JEN: *(Madly reading a beat-up soft cover, looks up.)* I'm not finished yet.

LILY: OH! AS I WAS SAYING: I–

ANA: Lily, you know, we have a rule about turning off cell phones before Book Club.

WILL: Book Club is just like the theater.

LILY: Oh Ana, no worries. My Kindle is on the fritz and I left my iPad charging at work. I just downloaded *Moby Dick* for free onto my cell.

WILL: Really?

LILY: It's easy and in the public domain.

ANA: I just like the feel of a real book: the paper, the cover.

LILY: But this is the future. *(To the camera.)* And this saves trees!

ANA: Right. As I was about to say: we could focus the whole conversation on the first line alone! Who is "Ishmael"?

LILY: Did you know Ishmael is the Biblical name of a social outcast and—

ROB: Wait. All I needed was to read the first line?

WILL: But, Rob, if you only read the first line, then you wouldn't know what happens at the end.

JEN: *(Blurts.)* Finished!

ROB: Oh, I know what happens. In the end, poor Moby Dick dies.

JEN: Not really, Rob. *(Beat.)* The ending is still very fresh for me.

ROB: Moby doesn't die?

WILL: The White Whale can never die.

LILY: He is God.

ANA: He is destiny.

JEN: He is nature.

ROB: Oh.

ANA: You didn't read the book, did you, Rob?

ROB: It's 615 pages dense and long… and I love animals.

ANA: Rob–

ROB: Seriously, I tried, Ana, I really tried.

ANA: Thank you for trying.

LILY: Will, I wasn't surprised that *Moby Dick* was your book choice.

ANA: Why is that, Lily?

LILY: It's just such an ambitious… and male book. Captain Ahab seeking revenge on the whale that destroyed his leg.

WILL: Thank you, Lily. Funny, his book got terrible reviews when it first came out. And now it's a great American classic.

JEN: I suppose people just thought of it as a popular adventure book.

ROB: How could this be popular? It's so long.

JEN: I learned so much from this book… About life. About people. About harpoons…

WILL: My favorite line was, "Better to sleep with a sober cannibal than a drunken Christian."

LILY: Which makes me wonder if there's a homosexual subtext, between Queequeg the Cannibal and Ishmael.

WILL: *(Beat.)* I don't think so.

LILY: Queequeg has to be gay.

ANA: Queequeg is not gay.

WILL: Queequeg is a cannibal.

LILY: Maybe a bi-curious cannibal?

LILY and JEN laugh.

ANA: This is an American classic, Lily.

LILY: I know! And this American classic is filled with homoerotic subtext.

JEN: Is there subtext in the title?

Everyone laughs varying degrees of laughter, less from ANA.

ANA: That's so funny. But "Dick" meant something different back then. Perhaps, we should deepen instead of broaden, don't you think?

ROB: Well, isn't Moby Dick a SPERM whale?

JEN snorts, she laughs so hard. This time, ANA is not amused.

ANA: Jen, we are trying to have a serious conversation here.

JEN: Sorry. I'm working too much and sleeping too little.

LILY: No matter, this book is a long beautiful ode to "man love."

WILL: Really?

LILY: Page 113, "Some old couples often lie and chat over old times till nearly morning. Thus, then, lay I and Queequeg—a cosy, loving pair." Isn't that homoerotic?

WILL: No. That is just roommate stuff. Right, Rob?

ROB: Right.

WILL: Rob and I were roommates in college.

LILY: Oh, I wondered how you guys got to be friends.

WILL: Rob was the handsome, athletic type from a very good family.

ANA: His grandfather was a brilliant scientist that helped invent the birth control pill!

ROB: My middle name is "Novum."

ANA: Will, on the other hand, was more hard-working and organized.

WILL: I liked making thematic window displays in my parent's little grocery store. Corn, corn flakes. Corn syrup.

ANA: A born museum curator.

LILY: Well, it's cool that two such different men can be so close.

WILL and ROB high-five.

ROB & WILL: Oh yeah!

LILY: It's refreshing to see a jock and a gay man as best friends.

The men are about to bump elbows or high-five again and freeze. Stunned pause.

ANA: Lily—Will is not gay.

LILY: *(Laughs.) That's a good one! (Laughs. Stops.)* Wait, you're serious?

JEN: Very serious.

LILY: *(Laughs a little.)* Really?

WILL: Lily, I am not gay.

LILY absorbs the fact, the room.

LILY: Oh Will, I'm sorry. *(Sees the camera.)* I am so sorry. I just—

ROB: Lily, why would you think Will is gay?

LILY: Ah… I don't… know… *(Looks around for help. JEN looks down at her hands.)*

WILL: Is it the way I dress?

LILY: No. That's–not–

ANA: I love the way you dress, Will.

LILY: It's very elegant.

WILL: Is it my voice?

LILY: Not at all!

ROB: You have a total guy voice, Will.

WILL: Or my love of literature–or musical theatre–?

LILY: Noooo!

ANA: Will, I'm sure Lily meant nothing of the sort.

LILY: Ana is right. And besides, everyone knows gay is cool. Very cool.

WILL: Not one of us is disparaging gayness in any form. I'm just curious what made you think I was gay.

LILY: Oh, I don't know what made me say that… Maybe it's because you are almost 40 years… young! And unmarried and I assumed…

WILL: Oh, so do you think Jen's gay too?

LILY: No!

WILL: So Jen's not cool enough to be gay?

LILY: That's not what I meant at all.

JEN: Hey! I'll have you know, I kissed a girl my sophomore year of college.

ROB & WILL: *(Look at LILY.)* Really?

LILY: Who didn't!

ROB & WILL: Really?

ROB and WILL turn hopefully to hear the same thing from ANA.

ANA: Lily, Will was my first real kiss.

LILY: Oh! Really?

WILL: Freshman year. We were each other's first real love.

ANA: Long walks by the river, picnics in the park,

WILL: We kissed under the elms.

ANA: We did.

WILL: Beautiful Ana was all mine, until this handsome
　　bastard stole her away and broke my heart. Right, buddy?

ROB: Right.

ANA: Rob and I fell for one another during crew practice.

ROB: Ana was my coxswain.

ANA: Something about the way Rob rowed really… rocked
　　my boat.

ROB: All I had to do was look at Ana's mouth… opening and
　　closing, telling… me… what to do.

WILL: They tried to hide it from me. Until I walked in on
　　them in the heat of lovemaking!

ANA: Oh God! I was mortified.

ROB: Will was so upset. He screamed at us, then threw a book
　　at me.

WILL: *Paradise Lost* by Milton.

ROB: In hardback. It knocked me out.

WILL: And then I turned to run for help and broke my nose against the door.

ANA: Things were so intense and passionate between us back then. We all found each other at the hospital, hurt and bruised, and I wept for the pain I caused these two wonderful men... whose friendship was torn apart because they both loved me. I vowed to myself that I would bring us back together by building something strong and beautiful which became our Book Club. And my men agreed.

WILL: *(Beat.)* I thought Book Club was my idea.

ANA: No, it was my idea.

WILL: Oh, because I thought–

ANA: Will, it was my idea that I shared with you, my book lover!

WILL: *(Flattered.)* Oh, Ana.

LILY: How inspiring! After all that heartbreak, you are all still friends.

JEN: It's a pretty amazing love story, huh?

ROB: Ana and I got married. Will was the best man.

WILL: At their ceremony, I read a gorgeous excerpt of *Paradise Lost.*

LILY: Who would have thought *Moby Dick* would bring out so much personal revelation?

ANA: *(From the end of the book.)* "Towards thee I roll, thou all-destroying but un-conquering whale; to the last I grapple with thee; from hell's heart I stab at thee; for hate's sake I spit my last breath at thee, thou damned whale!"

People clap.

WILL: God, I love Book Club!

ANA: Now honey, don't you wish you had read the book?

ROB: Maybe if I got to pick something I liked.

WILL: Ana has been taking your turn for the past five years, Rob.

ANA: Oh honey, I'm sorry! I thought you liked it that way.

ROB: I did. But I think I would like to take my turn back now.

ANA: Oh Rob! Really? *(Hugs him.)*

WILL: What do you want to read, buddy?

ROB: Something fun and exciting.

JEN: Can I suggest a new rule that it be less than 400 pages?

ROB: Absolutely!

ANA: It will be a window into your soul, Rob.

LILY: Rob, just pick a book and we will all read it with you.

ROB: Right now? I don't know what to pick right now!

ANA: Listen, honey. Jen has already selected her book for the next meeting, right?

JEN: *The Age of Innocence* by Edith Wharton. An American classic set in 1870s New York. 278 pages.

LILY: Nice choice, Jen!

WILL: Rob, that gives you two weeks to choose your book. And then we will all read yours. OK?

ROB: OK! Jen, I promise I'll read your book too.

ANA: We'll see…

JEN: That would be great!

LILY: Good night everyone. Thank you. The dip was great.

ANA: Don't mention it.

LILY: Again, Will. I'm sorry for my assumption about you.

WILL: Worry not, dear Lily. As you know, you can't judge a book by its cover.

LILY: I'll say.

WILL: You of all people should know that!

Beat. The whole room freezes.

LILY: Oh–Why? Because I'm… from Akron, Ohio?

WILL: No. No. Yes! But… I love… Akron, Ohio.

LILY: Me too! Some of my best friends are "Akron-Americans."

WILL: Oh, Lily… I'm sorry. I just put my foot in my mouth.

LILY: Will, I did the exact same thing too. And I'm sorry as well. *(They hug.)* Good night, Will.

WILL: Good night, Lily!

JEN: Will, can I have a ride?

WILL: Did you lose your keys again?

JEN: They're not lost. They're just not with me.

WILL: C'mon then! Thanks for everything, everybody. Bye, Ana, my love.

JEN: Thanks! Bye everyone!

Everyone dashes out. LILY looks at ANA and ROB.

ANA: Lily, that hug between you and Will is what Book Club is all about.

LILY: I'm sorry, I just really thought Will was gay!

ANA: Lily, I didn't want to embarrass Will, but the discomfort you sense from him is because he is still in love with me.

LILY: Omigoodness.

ANA: Rob and I have discussed it…

ROB: We have.

ANA: And there's nothing we can do but try to make Will feel as happy and comfortable as we can.

LILY: It's a testament to your friendship that Book Club works as well as it does.

ANA: Oh Lily. I see so much of myself in you. You are a great writer… and you're already so connected to the pulse of this city! You are heading straight for the top!

LILY: *(Laughs.)* I don't know about that. But thank you for your help and support. Good night, Ana. Good night, Rob

ROB: Good night, Lily.

LILY leaves.

ROB: *(Cont'd.)* Well, that went well!

ANA: Oh, I really hope so…

ROB: Your dip was great.

ANA: Thanks… but… I just… *(She looks at the camera lowers her voice.)* Oh forget it.

ROB: Is it because of the camera?

ANA: I'm sure Lars will edit this out.

ROB: OK. Then.

ANA: I mean that "Sperm whale" joke, Rob? Was that necessary?

ROB: Jen laughed!

ANA: And Lily's assumption about Will. And Jen arriving late. And Will offending Lily! Rob, what are the Danes going to think about us when they see that?!

ROB: You said we should be ourselves.

ANA: I mean "our better selves."

ROB: Our better selves?

ANA: Book Club is about elevating our conversation, our thoughts, our souls through great literature. And being brave and trying new things and allowing the world to see how reading improves our lives. This documentary means a lot to me.

ROB: Is that why you told everybody, in front of the camera, that I was a disappointment?

ANA: What? When? I would never say that about you!

ROB: After I said I would read *The Age of Innocence*–You said: "We'll see… "

ANA: Rob, I love you, but why do you come to Book Club and never read the books!? You are missing the whole point!

ROB: I think the books are just an excuse to hang out, eat and be… people.

ANA: Yes, but the best people you can be!!! *(Beat.)* Sorry, honey. It's really *my* problem not yours. I just need to be a stronger me and make my peace with it.

ROB: Ana, you wait and see! I am going to read *The Age of Innocence* if it's the last thing I do.

ROB storms off.

Lights shift.

Projection: ELSA JONES-EISENBLITZ, Literary Agent, New York, N.Y.

Spotlight on ELSA (played by PUNDIT or JEN.) She is wearing big eyeglasses, a shawl.

ELSA: Humans need five things… four of which we share with other animals: water, food, shelter and sex. The unique fifth thing humans need is story. The sixth thing is stories about sex—hell, I'm kidding!

But, seriously, there are like seven billion people that inhabit our planet, and every one of us has a story. Some, like my father, keep their story inside; most, like my mother, tell theirs to the neighbors, and a few like, two billion people, take the time to jot something down for posterity.

Writing a book is hard work. It takes heart. It takes discipline; it even sometimes takes, God help me, talent.

I can't even tell you how many millions of manuscripts are submitted each year, but it's a friggin' heartbreaking colossal number. And these are the facts. Of the millions and millions of manuscripts that are submitted each year only 250,000 are published. And out of the 250,000 books that are published, most Americans read an average of less than three. You do the math.

Writing a book takes courage. Getting it published takes luck.

But getting someone to read your book takes a friggin'
miracle.

Lights out.

Projection: *The Age of Innocence* by Edith Wharton.

ANA: Lars Knudsen has provided us with one or two talking
points. Let me open the envelope.

WILL: Practice for the Oscars, maybe?

ANA: Ah-ha! "What book had the deepest impact on you,
when you were young?"

Ad-lib murmurs and responses.

LILY: *Sounder* changed my childhood.

WILL: Oh, my God. *Sounder*!

LILY: Read it in fourth grade and I cried until snot plopped
on the pages. Life for a poor share-cropper was hard
enough, but did they have to kill his dog?

WILL: A brutal book.

JEN: That ending nearly killed me.

ANA: For me it was *Old Yeller*.

Everybody moans their appreciation.

LILY: It's wonderful how dead dogs bring the world together.

Everyone laughs.

ROB: *(Pause.)* When I was fifteen–

ANA: Honey, don't look at the camera.

ROB: When I was fifteen, I liked reading those books about the NFL... you know, they were this thin and they had a blurry picture of the player on it. My father was not happy. Junior, can't you read something serious? Something classic? Something British? Oh yeah, Dad?! How about *Tarzan of the Apes*?

After reading that book, something in me clicked. I volunteered at the local zoo and helped sweep the gorilla pavillion. You know what's amazing? Putting your hand up to the window and having a gorilla do the same thing. So human-like... I promised myself that when I grew up, I would move to Africa and work with baby gorillas.

JEN: I didn't know that.

ANA: Rob has a very big heart, you know.

ROB: Instead, I grew up, got married and went into pharmaceutical sales.

ANA: And he just got a fantastic promotion! Rob was offered a vice-president position in the company!

LILY: Wow, in this economy?

JEN: That's great!

ROB: We are a pharmaceutical company. Recession is great for depression. Will, what was your book?

WILL: *The Little House.* I remember the pictures very vividly. It was the true story of this cute little pink house that was in the middle of a field... and how the world encroached on it, and it became a little pink house shadowed by enormous skyscrapers and cowering beneath supersonic jets until... someone had the decency to scoop it up and put in a field where it could just be. It's a true story of the historical preservation society's heroic efforts to find a home for that house. And a clear indication of my early love for history.

JEN: I fell in love when I was fourteen. Hard. The kind of love that makes you jittery, that fills you with hope and despair all at once. I look for him in every guy I kiss: Heathcliff.

LILY: Heathcliff!

JEN: What an asshole! And I'll be damned if *Wuthering Heights* hasn't ruined me in some way.

ROB: I just don't get it.

JEN: Get what?

ROB: My company makes billions of dollars selling pills that make people feel less sad. And here you are, delighting in reading books that are full of heartbreak, despair and dead dogs.

LILY: You should read *Wuthering Heights*, Rob.

JEN: It breaks your heart in the best way.

ROB: Why not read something that makes us happy?

JEN: *Wuthering Heights* makes me happy. Nothing beats getting swept up like that… in the characters, in the story.

ANA: The beautiful lush language.

WILL: The breathless yearning.

LILY: And there's always the hope!!! The happy ending.

JEN: Exactly! That's the most painful part. That goddamn hope!!!

LILY: Hope is hell! And I love it!

WILL: Me too!

JEN: To hope! To hell! And to *Wuthering Heights*!

ROB: But you said *Wuthering Heights* kind of ruined you!!

WILL: I think Jen might be saying that her romantic notions have hurt her in the past.

JEN: *(Blurts.)* Ah, my scandal.

LILY: What scandal?

JEN: Can I have more wine, please?

ANA: Oh Jen, forget it! It happened so long ago… old news.

LILY: I'm sorry. I didn't mean to be nosy.

JEN: Oh God. Lily, I'm sorry. You are a part of our Book Club family. You should know.

ANA: Jen, no worries. Lily can Google it at home: alone.

JEN: But we are a community. Lily, remember some years ago the scandal involving a young legal intern and a certain married Senator? The total implosion of the State Senate? "The Mouse that Brought Down the House?"

LILY: Ohmigod! You were the mouse!

ANA: Jen… you really don't have to…

JEN: I left my job in disgrace; tax payers picketed the Senate, people were fired; his wife divorced him…

ANA: We try to never talk about it.

JEN: I lost everything. My heart. My job. My law school scholarship. And just when I thought there was no hope. I got a phone call from my old friend Will.

WILL: I said, "Jenny, get out of bed, and come to Book Club."

JEN: And I did. That phone call meant the world to me.

ANA: And we are so lucky to have Jen as a friend and Book Clubber. The end!

ROB: See? That's what I'm talking about! A happy ending!!

LILY: Jen, thank you for sharing.

JEN: Thank you.

WILL: Catharsis.

JEN: Now, Ana, if we could just stop and rewind the camera, before we go on.

ANA: Oh, Jen, no.

JEN: No?

ANA: Jen, that box it is in… it's locked. We can't touch the camera.

JEN: What?! I assumed, Ana, you would have control of it.

ANA: Me? Have control? Why would you think that?

JEN: Umm–I just–

ANA: Jen, didn't you read the release before you signed it?

JEN: *(Beat.)* Oh-my-God… Lars–Lars–edit out what I just said. Cut it! Please.

ANA: Jen–please don't talk to the camera.

WILL: Jenny, it's OK.

JEN: It's not. I was sharing with Lily. Not Lars! I can't… I don't want an audience in my life.

ANA: *(Gently.)* Audience? Do you see an audience?

All look out at the audience.

JEN: Guys, I don't think I want to be part of this film.

ANA: *(Pause.)* Jen, I love you and if you don't want to be a part of this film, I respect that.

JEN: Ana, thank you.

ANA: You will just have to find a time to meet up with us after Book Club.

JEN: What?

ANA: Or you can rejoin Book Club in three months after Lars' film is done.

ROB: What? No!

WILL: That's not what Ana means…

LILY: No Jen at Book Club?

WILL: Jenny, do you want to leave Book Club?

JEN: No. You know how much I love reading the books and how I look forward to discussing them with you. Ana, Book Club kind of saved my life.

ANA: I know, Jen. And it wouldn't be Book Club without you.

WILL: Book Club needs you!

ROB: Plus, I love your nachos and refried beans, Jen. *(Takes a bite.)*

JEN: You guys…

ANA: Nachos is such an original choice to complement a book like *The Age of Innocence.* What is your recipe for the refried beans?

JEN: You know… a can.

WILL: Please stay.

ROB: We need you. And your nachos.

ANA: You add crunch to our meetings.

LILY: And besides, *The Age of Innocence* is fantastic.

JEN: *(Sits.)* What the hell. I need to talk about this book.

LILY: I also loved the Scorsese movie. Michelle Pfeiffer and Daniel Day Lewis.

JEN: Me too!

ROB: Wait! There's a movie of this?… By Martin Scorsese?

WILL: *(ROB tries to break in a couple of times during WILL's speech.)* OK, Rob, let me fill you in. The book takes place in New York, in the late eighteen hundreds. Newland Archer is the main character. He's a stuffy, class-oriented snob that is about to marry this pretty, little, bland thing called May Welland. And he thinks he is happy, until he meets May's cousin, the exciting and exotic Countess Ellen Olenska, who is creating scandal by divorcing her husband, and living her life on her own terms. Archer is madly attracted to Ellen, forcing him to question all that he believes to be sacred and true–

ROB: I know that.

WILL: Oh. You do?

ROB: I read the book.

JEN: You did?

ANA: All of it, honey?

ROB: Yes, honey, all of it.

ANA: Rob! I'm so proud of you.

LILY: I loved *The Age of Innocence*! All that repressed passion stuffed into one haunted husband. It's excruciatingly painful and beautiful.

ROB: I hated *The Age of Innocence*.

JEN: What? Why?

ROB: It… troubled me. I couldn't sleep.

WILL: Rob, why did it bother you?

ROB: After reading this, I don't know, I wanted to, you know, scream. Or break something. I don't know, I guess… Listen… chapter thirty.

ROB opens the book.

ROB: *(Cont'd.)* "Never, in all the years to come, would May surprise him by an unexpected mood, by a new idea, a weakness, a cruelty or an emotion.

His wife had spent her poetry and romance on their short courting: the function was exhausted because the need was past.

He laid down his book and stood up impatiently; and at once she raised her head."

ANA decides to be MAY in what she feels is a delightful interpretation.

ANA: "What's the matter?"

ROB: "'The room is stifling: I want a little air.'

The mere fact of not looking at May, the fact of seeing a whole world beyond his world, cleared his brain and made it easier to breathe."

ANA: "Newland! Do shut the window. You'll catch your death."

ROB: *(Fires back.)* "'Catch my death!' he echoed; and he felt like adding: 'But I've caught it already… *(Discovery.)* I am dead. I've been dead for months and months.'"

WILL, JEN and LILY along the way realize this is not a game to ROB.

ANA: "Are you ill?"

ROB: "Poor May!"

ANA: "Poor? Why poor?"

ROB: "Because I shall never be able to open a window without worrying you… And I shall never be happy unless I can open the windows!"

"He paused, a man who longs for a change, and is yet too weary to welcome it. Something he knew he had missed… The flower of life." *(Beat.)* The flower of life.

ROB closes the book.

ANA: Thoughts? Impressions? Questions?

ROB slowly sinks to the floor as ANA is talking.

WILL: Rob, buddy, are you OK?

ROB: I don't think so.

ANA: Does your stomach hurt?

ROB: No. *(Rubs his chest.)*

WILL: Rob, is it your chest?

ANA: Your chest!

ROB: It's my heart.

WILL: YOUR HEART!!!!

ANA: What are your symptoms, honey?

ROB: Like something is… cracking.

LILY: Could it be a signs of… a panic attack? Or cardiac arrest?

ROB: *(Calmly.)* No. It's definitely not a heart attack.

ANA: Then what is it?

LILY: *(Pulls out her phone.)* Wikipedia MD will tell us.

WILL: You need some herbal tea.

WILL exits.

ANA: I should call our doctor.

ROB: Ana, I don't need a doctor.

LILY: Your computer. My phone is almost out of juice.

LILY exits.

ANA: You'll need my password. Rob–hang in there honey. Jen, look after him, please. *(Exits.)*

ROB: That book freaked me out! I'm so confused.

JEN: There. There.

ROB: Where is my flower of life, Jen? Where is my flower of life?

JEN: Rob, it's there. You have it.

ROB suddenly kisses JEN. With passion. It's a good sweet kiss for both of them.

ROB: Oh my God.

JEN: *(Shocked.)* Oh my God.

ROB: That was so sweet.

JEN: It was, but Rob, it didn't happen.

ROB: *(Opens his eyes.)* I am so sorry, Jen.

JEN: It's OK, Rob.

ROB: I don't do things like that. Ever.

JEN: I know. Forget about it. This. It didn't happen.

ROB: You're right. It did not happen.

Both JEN and ROB turn and see the camera and gasp.

JEN & ROB: *(Simultaneously.)* Oh-my-God!!!

ANA enters.

ANA: How's the patient, Jen?

JEN: I don't know!

ANA: What's the matter?

JEN: Heartburn! Rob has beartburn, right?

ROB: Yeah. Yeah. That's it.

ANA: Everyone, mystery solved. Rob has heartburn!

LILY enters.

LILY: That was third on the list.

ANA: Of course! Those canned refried beans!

JEN: I'm sorry.

WILL: I have some Pepto in my briefcase. I need a spoon.

ANA: I'll get a spoon.

LILY: I'll find Alka-Seltzer.

ANA: Lily—it's in the bathroom.

LILY, ANA and WILL exit. JEN and ROB are alone. They agitatedly gesture to camera.

ROB: Lars, listen! It was nothing!

JEN: Please! Cut! Cut! Cut!

ROB: Lars, for the love of God!!!!

LILY enters, as do WILL and ANA. ROB and JEN stop..

LILY: Alka-Seltzer

WILL: Pepto Bismol.

ANA: And an appropriately sized spoon.

WILL: This will make you feel so much better.

ANA: Pick your poison, honey.

ROB opens wide. A spoonful of Pepto then a swig of Alka-Seltzer.

ROB: I think I'm just going to lie here.

LILY: Do we need to cancel the rest of Book Club?

JEN: I think so. Yes!

ANA: Over heartburn? No!

WILL: After all that excitement I don't know if everyone is up for spending the night talking about wannabe lovers.

ROB moans and lies down.

JEN: Agreed.

ANA: Honey, Lars Knudsen needs footage. We can't let him down.

ROB: I don't want to let anybody down.

WILL: There is Cannes.

LILY: Well if we don't want to end early… did Lars send any more of those "talking points in an envelope"?

ANA: Great idea! There is one addressed to you, Lily.

LILY: To me?

LILY: *(Opens it.)* "Lily Louise Jackson, as the newest member in the Book Club. When and why did you join?" I was invited to join the Book Club… what, three months ago?

ANA: Yes, about then.

LILY: It was such a nice surprise. Moving to a new city is hard. I thought it might be nice to make some new friends beyond Facebook.

JEN: Lily, you were an inspired choice. I mean, Ana described you and brought your resumé.

ANA: Lily Louise Jackson. A Summa Cum Laude from Kenyon College.

WILL: And we voted to give you a trial run, no hesitation.

LILY: Oh, you voted on me?

ANA: Yes, we have a vetting process, you know.

LILY: I did not know that.

WILL: Well, we do.

LILY: Like affirmative action for Book Clubs?

ROB sits straight up.

LILY: *(Cont'd, laughs.)* GOTCHA! I'm just kidding!

ANA, JEN, WILL and ROB all laugh.

ANA: See?! Fresh! Irreverent. Keeping us on our toes. You passed with flying colors. Everyone loved you.

JEN: That's the night we read *Black Like Me*.

LILY: Which I found interesting.

WILL: Me too.

ANA: Yes, we like to read very diverse things. International writers. Writers of color.

LILY: *Black Like Me* was written by a white man.

ANA: *(Beat.)* Yes it was. But I've read *Love in the Time of Cholera* by Gabriel García Márquez.

WILL: *Native Son* by Richard Wright.

JEN: *The Color Purple* by Alice Walker, *Beloved* by Toni Morrison and *Devil in a Blue Dress* by... what's his name ...

LILY: Walter Mosely. You read all of those in Book Club?

JEN: No–

JEN and WILL look at each other worried.

WILL: Not in Book Club.

Pause.

ANA: Omigoodness. Please don't tell me we have only read dead white men in Book Club?

JEN: Edith Wharton is a dead white woman.

WILL: And we've read some white men that are alive.

ANA: Oh no! See Lily, this is why we need you, to keep us real.

WILL: It's a terrible oversight.

JEN: We must do... something!

LILY: Ladies, and gentlemen, calm down.

ANA: We just have to remedy the situation, immediately. We should just skip ahead and let Lily pick the book for next meeting.

ROB: But I was going to pick the next book. *Return of Tarzan*!

ANA: Rob, sweetheart, no! This Book Club is about respect, tolerance, and what's truly important: It's about real literature. Don't you think we should do the right thing and let Lily pick next?

ROB: Let's do the right thing. *(Lies back down.)*

Beat.

JEN: So Lily, the Book Club choice is yours.

ANA: Lily–Shake us up! Challenge us! Don't be scared to bring in literature that's provocative with a lot of "soul."

LILY: Really? Oh! OK! Provocative? With "soul"? *(Beat.)* How about *Twilight*?

ANA: *Twilight*?

WILL: *Twilight*??

JEN: Yeah! *Twilight*!

LILY: You know the bestseller about vampires?

ANA: Vampires...

LILY: I bet *Twilight* is full of "soul." Undead ones. *(She makes vampire gesture.)*

ANA: *(Uncomfortable beat.)* Fabulous

Lights change.

Projection: FRANK, Secret Service Agent, Washington, D.C.

FRANK can be played by WILL or PUNDIT in dark glasses.

FRANK: Book Clubs? Yeah, I know about Book Clubs. I've been in a Secret Service Book Club for fifteen years.

My favorite books are *A Farewell to Arms*, *The Old Man and the Sea* and *For Whom the Bell Tolls*, all by Ernest Hemingway.

The most important part of my life is Book Club. People come and go, but the Book Club stays. There are certain unalterable rules you must follow if you want Book Club to survive and thrive.

One: Trust no one. Everyone must be vetted by the Book Club. Sure so-and-so might be someone's best friend, but that doesn't mean he won't pose a serious threat to Book Club.

Two: Take no prisoners. If a rogue element does somehow infiltrate Book Club, you must be ruthless, absolutely ruthless, in removing him

Three: Protect your leader. Book Club will collapse without the firm hand of authority and rule of law.

Ignore these rules at your Book Club's peril.

You have been warned.

***Projection: Twilight* by Stephenie Meyer**.

Lights on the Book Club: LILY, ROB, ANA, JEN and WILL.

ANA: Before we talk about *Twilight*, I want to share something very important. Being with all of you has given me the opportunity to make a big change in my life.

ROB: What kind of change?

ANA: I have decided to take a leave of absence from my column.

ROB: Honey, you're telling me this now? With everyone? In front of the camera?

ANA: Rob, I thought you would be delighted by the surprise. You have that new promotion and raise! Besides it's just a short leave of absence. This documentary has made me realize I work too much at the paper. I need to make room for other life things.

ROB: Oh honey! *(Kisses her.)* Let's have a baby! A sweet baby that is as smart and pretty as you!

JEN: So you two are thinking about a baby!!!?

ROB & ANA: *(Simultaneously.)* Yes! / No.

ROB: I thought you said you really wanted a baby.

ANA: I do but I'm taking a creative leave. I need to explore new things.

ROB: A baby is very new.

ANA: Honey, right now is not the right time.

ROB: Ana, we are not getting any younger…

ANA: Rob, I don't think this is the place… *(Refers to the camera.)*

ROB: Oh, I thought this was the perfect place to make huge personal life decisions!

ANA: Rob, can I talk to you over here? Off camera? Everyone, carry on.

ROB follows ANA "off camera." Everyone sits awkwardly. The focus is on the Book Club listening to the private conversation off camera. They can hear everything.

ANA: *(Offstage.)* Rob, what is wrong with you?

ROB: *(Offstage.)* I want a baby. I want to take care of something… smaller… and bigger than just us. I want the flower of life.

ANA: *(Offstage.)* Rob, we are in the middle of Book Club.

ROB: *(Offstage.)* Are we going to have a baby or not?

ANA: *(Offstage.)* Of course… just not right this second.

ROB: *(Offstage.)* I don't think you want one.

ANA: *(Offstage.) I love babies! LOVE THEM. Ask anyone. (Comes back into the room with ROB.)* Jen, Will, Lily. Don't I love babies?

WILL: Doesn't everybody?

ROB: Loving babies and wanting to have one are two different things.

LILY: You know, kids aren't for everyone.

WILL: That's what I tell my staff every time they want to create a touch-and-feel vase exhibit for children.

JEN: *(Blurts.) I really want to have a baby. (Covers her mouth.)*

LILY: Wow, Jen.

Beat.

ANA: Oh Jen! Are you dating someone again?

JEN: No. I'm not. And time is ticking… and here I am: dreaming of being a mom…

WILL: You would be a terrific mom!

JEN: I know. But I haven't found my Heathcliff!

LILY: Have you thought of a sperm bank?

JEN: A sperm bank? Oh. No. It sounds too sterile and impersonal.

LILY: My cousin used one! I helped her read through all the potential dad profiles. It was like sperm-bank speed dating. And now she has a beautiful baby boy.

JEN: I've always imagined my life with children.

ROB: I love horsing around with my nieces and nephews!

WILL: Jenny, you would be a wonderful mother.

JEN: Thank you, guys.

ANA: I am in awe. Of course Jen would be... very loving. It's just it is so much work. Good mothers are organized, and firm, and consistent.

JEN: I think lots of good moms embrace the chaos of kids. Kids need love more than anything.

ROB: I would LOVE to be a stay at home dad.

ANA: Rob, I'm not against having children, just not right now. Jen, I am so proud of you but I am so concerned; what would you do when you are alone, and the kid is crying and you can't find your keys? How will you cope? Prozac helps with your depression, but it won't change your baby's diapers.

All are suddenly deeply aware of the camera. Pause.

ANA: *(Cont'd.)* I'm so sorry.

ROB: We should talk about this later, Ana. You know, without an audience.

WILL: I think it would be great to get to the book. Now.

LILY: *(Holds up her Kindle.) Twilight* by Stephenie Meyer!

The doorbell rings.

WILL: The doorbell!

ANA: Who could that be, at this time?

JEN: No! Oh no! I can't believe it. He showed up.

LILY: Who showed up?

JEN: Alex. This guy in my building. We were in the laundry
   room in the basement and he… he was reading *Twilight*!

Pause.

WILL: Jenny—you know—that's not the way we do things.

JEN: I'm sorry. He was reading the book and he looked so
   sad. I blurted out the invitation and then I just couldn't
   take it back.

ANA: Oh, Jen.

WILL: Jenny, he could be an axe murderer for all we know.

LILY: He can't be all bad. He was reading the book selection.

WILL: That's exactly why I am concerned.

LILY: Is he cute?

JEN: He's not my type, but he's interesting. He had a lot of
   smart things to say about… vampires.

ANA: Oh no.

JEN: The poor guy just broke up with his girlfriend.

LILY: Oh, no.

Doorbell rings again.

JEN: I need to open that door.

ANA & WILL: WAIT!

JEN: I just invited him. On an impulse. That's all.

WILL: He has not been vetted by the group and it is just inappropriate to put us in this position.

ANA: Jen, he's going to have to come back another day.

LILY: That's silly, if he's read the book.

ROB: What does it matter if he has read the book!?

Doorbell rings.

JEN: I thought you would like him.

LILY: Oh this is ridiculous. There are five of us and only one of him. What harm can this man do?

ANA: Lily, you are right!

Light on ALEX. He enters.

ALEX: Book Club, I presume?

ANA: Everyone, this is Jen's friend, Alex.

ALEX: We are laundry mates. Hi, Jen.

JEN: Hi, Alex.

ANA: I'm Ana Smith. Welcome to my home and my Book Club.

WILL: Our Book Club.

ALEX: So this is the Book Club? It's not what I expected. At all.

LILY: *(Laughs and goes to shake his hand.)* Hello, Alex. I'm Lily.

ALEX: Hello, Lily

LILY: And this is Rob, Ana's husband. And this is Will.

ALEX: Hey.

ROB: Hey.

WILL: Hello.

ALEX: Hello, Book Club.

ANA: Thank you Lily, for the introductions.

ALEX: So no one here is a vampire?

ANA: God, no!

ALEX: There's always someone in a group wanting to suck the life out of someone.

LILY laughs. ALEX notices the camera.

ALEX: Whoa what's that?

JEN: Oh that's the bug-eyed camera I was telling you about.

ANA: Our Book Club is the subject of a Lars Knudsen documentary.

ALEX: Lars Knudsen! Impressive. *(Waves.)* Hi, Lars!

WILL: Please do not look at the camera!

ALEX: *(Looks at the audience.)* Oh. *(Shuns his face.)* OK.

ANA: Just try to forget it's there.

LILY: Please have a seat, Alex.

ALEX: How about *Twilight*? Did *Twilight* make you tingle all over?

LILY: It certainly stirred some feelings…

ANA: Excuse me?

WILL: Is that an appropriate question to ask on a first... Book Club?

JEN: Lily, it totally made me tingle, too!

ROB: Really?

ANA: Rob didn't read the book!

WILL: Lucky Rob.

LILY: OK, let me fill you in. A young seventeen-year-old girl, Bella Swan, moves to the rainy town of Forks in the state of Washington to live with her father. She describes herself as clumsy and ordinary.

ALEX: But all the boys in school, even the elusive, hyper-handsome Edward Cullen, seem interested in her.

LILY: That's right!

ALEX: Edward is attracted to Bella because the scent of her blood beckons him.

LILY: You see: Edward Cullen is a vampire.

WILL: A vegetarian vampire–

ROB: So that's why we had tofu for dinner.

WILL: And he hungers for Bella–to go to prom with him.

ROB: Prom? How can a vampire go to high school?

WILL: He's been seventeen for a hundred years.

ROB: But doesn't the sun kill vampires?

LILY: No, the sun makes Edward sparkle.

ALEX: Like glitter.

ROB: You're making this up.

JEN: Actually the author, Stephenie Meyer, made it up.

ALEX: Apparently, not all vampire cultures are the same.

ANA: There is NOTHING cultured about this book.

WILL: Amen.

LILY: Edward loves Bella but also yearns to drink her blood. And she loves him. But they can't make love…

ALEX: Because he's scared that in the heat of passion, he would lose control and… eat her.

LILY looks down at her Kindle and perhaps reads a passage from the book Maybe the three things of which Bella is certain. JEN sighs loudly in response to the passage.

WILL: Well, I'll just say this. I thought this book was dreadful. No action, poorly written. It's sexist and stupid. The heroine is a love-sick girl willing to give everything up for a vampire boy.

ANA: *(Agreeing with WILL)* Just look at how Edward is described in chapter thirteen.

Perhaps ANA reads aloud the passage where Bella admires Edward while lying in the meadow. Perhaps JEN, LILY and ROB sigh in response to the passage.

WILL: Ana, I highlighted the same ridiculous paragraph!

ANA: This is certainly not literature.

ALEX: Oh, and what makes something literature?

ANA: Not vampires! Not poor writing. Not poor plot. This is trivial!

LILY: Since when is the pursuit of love trivial, Ana?

ALEX: Your point about *Twilight* not being literature is interesting, Annie.

ANA: It's not Annie. It's not Anna. It's Ah-nuh.

ALEX: Ah-nuh, gotcha. I know oodles about books. I am a professor of comparative literature.

ROB: You are a professor?

ALEX: Up for tenure this year. And guess what? The woman of my dreams dumped me at the altar. It was very dramatic. You want to know why she dumped me?

ANA, LILY, ROB, JEN & WILL: Why?

ALEX: Because of a book: "Alex," she said, "You are NOTHING LIKE EDWARD CULLEN." And I said "Edward… who?" And she said, "That's exactly your problem. You have lost your passion. You have no clue."

JEN: Oh, I'm sorry.

ALEX: And she was right. I have lost my passion. I have no clue! I am completely out of touch. *Twilight* is a phenomenon. It has sold over 100 million copies and been translated into thirty-seven languages and yet, what did I know about Bella Swan and Edward Cullen? Nothing!!! Have you heard of *Fifty Shades of Grey*–???

JEN & LILY: *(Look at each other.)* Maybe…

ALEX: Well, that bestseller was inspired from *Twilight* fan fiction. And yet what do I know about inner goddesses and sadomasochist sex contracts? Apparently, not enough! And what's District 12 and who's Katniss and why play a *Hunger Game*? More than 350 million *Harry Potter* books have been sold worldwide, and what can I tell you about Hogwarts? Squat! I've never cracked open a Mary Higgins

Clark, a John Grisham or a Tom Clancy paperback. Never.

LILY: Really?

ALEX: And I am a professor of comparative literature!

LILY: Did you know romance is the most popular genre in modern literature? That Harlequin sells around four books a second!

ALEX: I am willfully oblivious to so much.

WILL: In this case, I would say willful oblivion is a very smart choice.

ANA: Just because millions of people like these books doesn't mean they're good. Popularity is not quality.

LILY: So you think ignoring what millions of people read or think is better?

WILL: This is a free country. If I read *Ulysses* instead of *Harry Potter*… that is my choice.

ANA: You have not read *Ulysses*, Will.

WILL: *(Icy.)* But I could!

JEN: Well, I've read all seven of the *Harry Potter* books.

LILY: Me too.

ROB: I love the *Harry Potter* movies.

ANA: I am proud to say I have not succumbed at all.

ALEX: And that is precisely my problem. What I think I am trying to say… is that a cultured person… a truly cultured person is connected–to the culture around him. A truly cultured person is… curious. You don't have to always like it… but you should try to experience it.

ANA: Popular culture is about entertainment. I am talking about enlightenment.

ALEX: A truly cultured person reads Salman Rushdie and Danielle Steel. A truly cultured person sees *La Traviata*, *Swan Lake* and *American Idol*; a truly cultured person listens to Bach and Beyoncé!!!!

LILY: It's terrible. I've never been to the opera.

JEN: Me neither.

ALEX: I have the best job in the world. My work is to read and talk about books all day! But reading stopped giving me any pleasure. How horrible is that? I lost my curiosity. I lost my connection. Now, I want that feeling... back! And how do I do that??

ROB: Tell me: how?

ALEX: I'll tell you how: *Twilight*.

ROB: Really? *(Picks up the book and starts to read it.)*

ANA: You cannot be serious! *Twilight* is not literature any more than ketchup is a vegetable.

ALEX: *Twilight* is the reason my girlfriend dumped me at the altar. And now I understand why. *Twilight* touched something primal in her; it made her want to feel passion, mystery and experience love that is worth undying for.

WILL: See? It's a terrible harmful book.

ALEX: Today, on campus, one of my students, Ming Woo, a very shy girl, who never speaks in class, interrupted my *Twilight* reading to tell me how much she loved the entire series. She told me that she was a TWI-HARD, which is code for a die-hard *Twilight* fan and she was TEAM JACOB.

LILY: Team Jacob! Yeah!

JEN: I'm Team Edward all the way.

LILY and JEN do a momentary mock vampire/werewolf hiss.

ALEX: Suddenly, I had a common language, a connection, with this quiet teenaged kid I never had before. And as she delved into the virtues of Jacob the werewolf vs. Edward Cullen the vampire, it hit me: My God, maybe Edward Cullen is this century's version of Heathcliff!

LILY & JEN: HEATHCLIFF!!!

ANA & WILL: NO!!!

ALEX: We can debate all night on whether *Twilight* is good or bad… but *Twilight* is an important book.

ANA: Forgive me, Alex, for being a culture snob, but a few of us have to make sure there are standards. I for one don't want future generations to walk through the Museum of American Antiquities and think that the full essence of who we were as a people is McDonalds happy meals, *American Idol* and *Twilight*.

WILL: God, no.

ALEX: You know, Ana, I swore never to be part of a silly Book Club like this one! But this is great! This silly Book Club will be the very thing that reminds me of why I fell in love with books in the first place. Because right now, I don't love books, I don't love reading, and I think… I don't love anything anymore…

Silence. JEN's cellphone goes off with a very hip, popular tune like something by Lady Gaga or Carly Rae Jepsen.

JEN: My phone! Oh God, sorry! *(She turns it off.)*

ALEX: Sorry. I haven't been quite myself.

LILY: Wow, Alex, I'm glad you came. That's an amazing story.

ALEX: Thank you, Lily. *(Downs the wine.)* I'm glad I came too. A thousand pardons. I hope I didn't ruin the evening. Jen, thank you so much for inviting me. All of you, thank you for having me. Ana, your house is… perfect. Lily, thank you for selecting the book. *Twilight* feels like destiny. *(Another connection with LILY.)* I should go.

ANA: Yes, perhaps you should.

ALEX: Goodbye.

WILL: Goodbye.

JEN: Goodbye, Alex.

LILY: It was nice meeting you, Alex.

ALEX: Just out of curiosity. What is your next book?

ANA: I really think Will had a terrific idea and that *Ulysses* by James Joyce would be the perfect book for us. Don't you?

Long pause.

JEN: It's kind of long, isn't it? Like 900 pages.

LILY: I thought the book had to be 400 pages or less.

ROB: Is there a movie?

ANA: My friends, *Ulysses* is a masterpiece. It is ranked first on the list of 100 best novels of the 20th century.

WILL: I know we should read *Ulysses*, but is two weeks enough time?

ALEX: Oh! Well if you are looking for a book that is under 400 pages, you can read in two weeks… and has lots of history…

WILL: History?

LILY: Yes?

ALEX: Why don't you read that old bestseller by Dan Brown: *The Da Vinci Code*? I hear it's fast and fun!

WILL: *The Da Vinci Code*?

ALEX: Have you read it, Will?

WILL: No, I have not.

ALEX: Me neither! But it's supposedly the most "popular book in the world." You should read that!

LILY: That's a great idea, Alex.

JEN: I already have it on my bookshelf.

ANA: Thank you for your input, Alex. But you are not a member of my Book Club–

WILL: *(Under his breath.)* Our Book Club–

ANA: And we've already selected *Ulysses*.

LILY: But Ana–it's not your turn. It's Rob's turn.

ROB: And I don't want to read *Ulysses*.

ANA: It's an amazing piece of work.

ROB: It's just not the right time, Ana.

JEN: How about *The Da Vinci Code*, Rob?

ROB: I don't know what I want!!

ANA: Of course you don't.

LILY: Well, I would like to read *The Da Vinci Code.*

JEN: Me too.

WILL: Well, I suppose it can't hurt; we only have two weeks. And the rule is 400 pages or less.

ANA: Fine! If that is what the Book Club wants then we will read *The Da Vinci Code.*

ALEX: I should go. I promise I will be much better behaved next time.

LILY: Great.

WILL: What–wait!!

ROB: Next time?

ANA: No–Alex, wait–you should know–

LILY: That we really look forward to seeing you here in two weeks!!!

JEN: Yes, we do.

ANA is shocked speechless.

ALEX: I'll be back with bells on! Thank you. I'm now reading *Search for Love* by Nora Roberts... It's quite the page-turner.

ALEX exits. LILY and JEN are giddy. WILL and ANA are horrified.

JEN: Omigod.

LILY: Oh-my-God!

WILL: Oh–MY–GAWD!

ANA: That was… just… just… *(Shivers.)*

JEN: Ana, you look so pale.

ROB: Like a vampire.

ANA: What just happened?

WILL: That man… I just don't know what to say.

JEN: Wow.

ROB: What's WOW about that guy?

LILY: I thought Alex was great. I honestly thought this was our best Book Club ever.

WILL: You can't be serious.

JEN: He's smart.

LILY: And he's cute.

ROB: I thought he was weird.

ANA: But Lily, You must admit, he was a little out there. A little intense.

LILY: Isn't that the point?

ANA: Of course, of course, but intense in a… comfortable way.

JEN: Comfortably intense?

WILL: Fine, I'll say it! Alex was annoying.

ANA: So annoying.

LILY: I thought he was interesting.

ANA: That's interesting, because I found him intensely annoying!

JEN: *(Blurts without regret.)* But isn't intensely annoying a prerequisite for Book Club?

Oops. All heads snap to JEN. Pause. Everyone looks at the camera.

ANA: You know, we should just stop this conversation before any of us say anything we regret. If there's one thing of which I am certain it is that THAT man does not belong in our Book Club.

WILL: Any man that has so little regard for books should not come to Book Club.

LILY: He's a comparative lit professor.

WILL: Which shows a self-loathing that I think is beyond comprehension.

ANA: People, there is no need to discuss this, because he's not coming back.

JEN: I thought Alex was great!

ANA: I'm surprised we feel so differently about this.

JEN: I am too.

Pause.

LILY: Well, isn't there a vote?

WILL: Now you want rules?!

LILY: What's the big deal?

WILL: The big deal is respect!

JEN: You know, if Will feels this strongly about it, we should just... forget it.

LILY: You're right, Jen.

Beat.

WILL: Oh, so now I'm Dictator Will: intolerant, inflexible.

ANA: Nobody said that.

LILY: But Will, if we don't vote…

WILL: That's not the kind of man I am! Let us vote!

ALEX bursts in.

ALEX: Hello again.

Everyone is startled.

ALEX: *(Cont'd.)* Sorry, didn't mean to surprise you. I forgot my book.

Silence.

ALEX: *(Cont'd.)* I'm sorry. Did I interrupt something?

All break into conversation kind of simultaneously overlapping.

LILY: Yes.

ANA: No.

JEN: Just wrapping up…

WILL: Talking about the weather.

ROB: The book.

ALEX: *(Beat.)* You were all talking about me, weren't you?

LILY: *(Long pause.)* Well, yes, Alex, actually, we were talking about you.

ANA: We were just discussing whether you would fit into Book Club.

JEN: I'm sorry, Alex. I didn't know this would be so uncomfortable.

ALEX: Don't be sorry, Jen. And I would very much like to join Book Club, Ana.

LILY: He wants in.

ALEX: Yes, I do!

ANA: Ever since I started this Book Club–

WILL: We started this Book Club–

ANA: We have had a vetting process followed by a group vote.

ALEX: And?

LILY: We were about to vote before you walked in.

ALEX: Ah, a jury of my peers. May I watch?

WILL: This is a private affair. I don't think that's necessary.

ALEX: Private? But there's a camera!

WILL: Shh! Don't look at it! We are supposed to be acting completely unaware.

ROB: Like gorillas in the mist.

ALEX: *(Beat.)* Democracy is about transparency, isn't it?

Pause.

LILY: Well, for me, if there's a vote. I vote YES for Alex.

WILL: *(Beat.)* I love you, Lily, but I must vote my heart. I vote NO.

JEN: I vote yes.

Beat.

ANA: Jen, don't you love Book Club?

JEN: I think I love Book Club more than you do, Ana. And I think Alex will be good for us.

ANA: I love this Book Club more than you can imagine. No! I vote NO.

ALEX: That's two to two.

Everybody slowly turns to ROB. Beat.

ROB: Oh Shit!

Lights out.

A 'pause' symbol is projected on the screen.

END OF ACT I

Act II

The 'pause' symbol is still on the screen. The 'play' symbol replaces it.

Projection: SAM W. THOMPSON, Stock Manager for Wal-Mart, Amarillo, Texas.

Spotlight on PUNDIT or ROB wearing a blue Wal-Mart vest with a nametag and smiley-face button.

SAM: I can say without doubt that Book Clubs are truly an economic phenomenon and Wal-Mart is a proud participant, feeding the nation's hunger for books. Our pricing policies enable most families to be able to own and enjoy novels, biographies and bestsellers. And the numbers speak for themselves: over a million copies sold of *The Da Vinci Code, Harry Potter*, can't keep him on the shelf. *The Chicken Soup* books sell like hot cakes.

And you know, not only do we encourage America to read, we encourage our employees by offering them a significant employee discount. I do believe we might have some intra-Wal-Mart Book Clubs, where employees from all Wal-Marts in a twenty-five mile radius get together to discuss novels. And let me say something that I have no way of qualifying, but I believe that employees find these Book Clubs so satisfying that it has made the issue of unions completely irrelevant in our organization.

Beat.

My favorite book? A personal question, no sure, I'm happy to address that… Just remember… not to judge a book by its cover. My favorite book… I would have to say is: well, I'll say it: *Lolita* by Vladimir Nabokov. Why? His use of language, humor, his ability to take the most horrid of situations and find a voice of humanity. Each turn of the phrase lands you in an unexpectedly original yet real place.

Pause.

No, I'm afraid Wal-Mart does not carry *Lolita*.

Projection: *The Da Vinci Code* by Dan Brown.

LILY: Five-four-three-two-and it's 7p.m.!

ALEX: Hello, America. *(To the camera.)* Hello, Copenhagen!

ANA: You are ruining Lars Knudsen's fine film. You are ruining our Book Club.

ALEX: We just got started.

ROB: Alex, she's talking to me.

JEN: We agreed to let Alex join us just one more time, and see what happened.

ROB: I didn't vote. I didn't break the tie. I thought we should try to work it out,

ANA: Argh! We should have made it unanimous rule.

LILY: I think Rob's non-vote forced us to come up with a good compromise.

ANA: A one-time compromise.

LILY: So are we going to be adults about this? Or–

ANA: I'm so upset. I haven't been able to sleep.

ROB: Is there any food tonight?

ANA: Your "non-vote." His non-book. My non-food.

ALEX: Um yeah… well… I can order pizza.

ROB: I love pizza.

ALEX: And I have some *(looks in his pocket)* gum for everyone while we wait.

ALEX: So? How about *The Da Vinci Code* by Dan Brown.

ANA: Oh God, help me.

ALEX opens the book.

ALEX: Let's just start at the beginning. We meet the curator in the grand gallery and also the attacker.

Perhaps ALEX reads a bit from the introduction of the curator and gallery. Also perhaps the bit describing the attacker.

WILL: An albino!

ANA: Or the Easter Bunny–

ALEX: So what did you think of the book?

Beat.

LILY: Alex… I am so happy that you are here and I really really wanted to like this book…

ALEX: But…

LILY: It's very… plot driven, isn't it?

JEN: And the characters… well… they aren't real people, are they?

ANA: The language is flat and lifeless. It felt like I was reading two-dimensional movie. Not a real book.

ROB: Good because I saw the movie instead.

ANA: This is Book Club, Rob!

ROB: I like Tom Hanks. And it's the same story isn't it? And instead of investing twenty hours, I just used two. And you said so yourself, the book felt like a movie.

ANA: A movie is never better than a book.

ALEX: *(To the camera.)* Lars, what do you think about that?

ANA looks at the camera and annoyed at ALEX.

ANA: What I mean is film cannot capture a whole book. Even if a book is—

WILL: I LOVED IT!!

ANA: Will?

WILL: I loved *The Da Vinci Code.* I loved every gasp-inducing, page-turning second in this book. I loved it so much I read it twice. I loved it so much, I want to go on a tour and see all the historic sites he talked about.

ANA: Will, are you all right?

WILL: Alex, this book. If I had read this book… ten years ago.

ANA: A lot of books have history in them, Will.

WILL: It's not just the history. It's not just the artifacts… although they are magnificent… but it's something more than that.

ROB: What?

WILL: There are secrets everywhere. The truth… is out there … hidden in plain sight.

JEN: Will, do you really think there are conspiracies?

WILL: Don't you?

JEN: I think conspiracies require a lot of organization and I don't see how—

WILL: Jenny, some of us thrive on organization. Some of us have everything tucked away exactly the way we think it should be. And yet, everyone is keeping secrets.

LILY: Isn't that a little paranoid, Will?

ALEX: Well, someone IS watching us...

Everyone looks at the camera.

WILL: Exactly. I mean that camera... do we really know Lars Knudsen is who he says he is?

ANA: He's a famous director!

WILL: *(To the camera.)* Lars Knudsen, who are you, really?

ANA: Will, please stop talking to the camera.

LILY: Will is right. Is anyone who they say they are?

ANA: Of course. I am Ana Smith!

WILL: But weren't you Annie Gomez Krapowsky before you married Rob? Huh? Huh?

ALEX: You were an Annie.

ANA: That's hardly a secret.

WILL: All of us keep secrets... from each other. From ourselves. What are those secrets? What are your secrets?

Beat. WILL looks around at each person. ANA looks for lint on her blouse, LILY checks her phone, ROB and JEN look at each other and away.

WILL: *(Cont'd.)* Look at page five. The curator realizes that if he dies no one would know the truth and that horrifies him. He needs to pass on the secret, needs to find a way ...

Perhaps WILL reads the segment about the importance of the truth aloud.

Suddenly, WILL kisses ROB.

ANA, LILY & JEN: Will!

ANA: Oh MY God!

JEN: Oh my God.

ANA, LILY & JEN: Oh my GOD!

ROB: Will, buddy–

WILL: Rob, you are the only reason I want to come to Book Club.

ANA: He is the only reason?!

WILL: And the books. But I cannot live a lie any longer. I want you to know, Rob.

My secret is that I LOVE YOU.

Shocked silence.

ALEX: Rob, how do you feel about what Will just said?

ROB: Will. Thanks, but.

WILL: I know it's impossible. You don't need to love me back. But I want you to know: Rob, I've secretly loved you since freshman year.

ANA: That can't be true!

WILL: Alas, Ana it is. I'm in love with you, Rob… because you are you… and because I am… I am…

ANA: Will–

LILY: Oh my GOD! Will, you are gay!

WILL: I am? *(Beat. He looks at JEN.)*

JEN: Willy, I think maybe so...

WILL: I am? *(Pause.)* Oh my... Oh my... Oh my. *(He sits stunned.)* I think I might be gay.

ANA: Will, I know how private and discreet you are and just because you are under some pressure... I just don't want you to regret anything... or commit to something that isn't really true. Will, your parents may see this documentary one day.

WILL: Mom and Pop?

ANA: Yes... working in their little grocery store... think of them

WILL: Hey, Mom and Pop. Guess what? *(Stands up.)* I'm GAY! I'm GAY!

He stops and starts to cry with relief.

ROB: Hey, buddy, it's OK.

JEN: I am so proud of you, Will. You are glorious!

LILY: You are beautiful.

WILL: Alex, thank you. *The Da Vinci Code* revealed the secret truth of my life.

ALEX: My pleasure, Will.

WILL: I vote we keep the professor.

JEN & LILY: Yeah!

WILL: TEAM ALEX!

ANA: No! Will–please... don't–

ROB: Will, did you just smell the flower of life?

WILL: Yes! And I must smell some more.

ANA: I hate that Edith Wharton book!

WILL: Rob, buddy, we should read your book!

ANA: What?

ROB: My book?

WILL: Yes, let's read *Return of Tarzan*.

ANA: No!

ROB: Really? You would do that for me?

JEN, LILY & WILL: Yes!

ROB: Thanks.

ALEX: *Return of Tarzan* it is!

LILY: Wow,

JEN: I'm so happy for you, Will.

WILL: Thank you!

ROB: I'm so weirdly happy too. Aren't you, Ana?

ANA: Of course… I always knew. I mean… it's so obvious.

LILY: But Ana you always thought Will was still in love with you!

ALEX: Really?

WILL: Ana?

ANA: You must have all misunderstood me.

LILY: Ana, you said Will loved you. *(Whispers.)* It's on film.

ANA looks at the camera.

WILL: Ana, I wanted to believe that too, But the secret truth is—it was always Rob.

ANA: *(Beat.)* I think I need to lie down.

ROB: Are you feeling OK?

ANA: My chest… it feels funny.

She exits, and ROB follows her out.

WILL: God have mercy, I'm gay.

JEN: Oh Will, I've been waiting for this day for so long!

JEN and WILL hug and weep.

WILL: *(Cries.)* I'm so happy!

ALEX: Is Book Club always like this?

LILY: Absolutely!

Lights shift.

Projection: Carl Banks, Book Dealer, Bay State Correctional Center, Framington, Massachusetts.

Played by PUNDIT or ALEX in an orange jumpsuit.

CARL: Here in the big house. We have a different sort of currency. Long days here, in the joint. And everyone is looking for some kind of release.

They call me "The Bookend." It goes like this. First three chapters, I am able to provide for free. You like that and want more, well… the next three will cost you three cigs. Hooked and need another fix? Well chapters seven to nine will be a whole pack. And the book junkies… they come and beg for the last chapters. Ha! That's where the price jacks up to full chocolate bar. And that's when the craziness begins, the begging, the threats, the altercations.

Shoot, one punk is in solitary today for perpetrating on my person to cut me if I didn't tell him the ending to *Presumed Innocent* by Scott Turow.

I protect myself and I do not read one word from those books. It's simple freakonomics. If you want to stay safe… never dabble in what you deal.

Projection: *The Return of Tarzan* by Edgar Rice Burroughs.

ANA: Everyone, I want to apologize for my… resistance the last couple of get-togethers. I want to be better and stronger than that. And I will be.

JEN: Ana, it's OK. You don't have to apologize to us.

ANA: But I do. You know, I think I was a little naïve when I said that all of this, the camera, the extra reading… wouldn't have an effect on us.

LILY: We've read a lot of books.

JEN: Yes.

ANA: And good books. Mostly. But I will be the first to admit that there were moments in the last weeks when I wasn't enjoying Book Club AT ALL. But I got an email from Lars Knudsen that he is really delighted with what he has seen so far.

ROB: Delighted?

ANA: Yes, he said Book Club was surprisingly "juicy."

JEN and ROB look at each other in panic.

JEN: Oh God. Did he talk about editing things out?

ANA: On the contrary; he wants more.

Panicked, JEN and ROB, behind ANA and the rest of the Book Club's back, secretly signal to LARS to cut things.

71

LILY: *(She claps.)* Fabulous! Let's give Lars more. Sundance, here we come!

ANA: We'll see. And Alex, Lars specifically told me to thank you for your release.

ALEX: *(To the camera.)* No. Thank you, Lars Knudsen.

ANA: He is planning on wrapping this all up in the next two or three sessions.

ROB: *(Dispirited.)* Awesome.

LILY: That soon? I think it's been kinda fun having old Lars with us.

ANA: Well, I for one will be grateful for all of us to return to our everyday, lovely normal lives and start having Book Club like it was.

JEN: Me too.

LILY: Ana, you are human, like the rest of us.

ANA: So human, really. I am. And Alex, I want to extend a personal apology to you.

ALEX: You do?

ANA: I'm just a little territorial; I am so deeply loyal to my Book Club family. I am afraid I may have come across as a tad unfriendly.

ALEX: I didn't notice.

ANA: We both know that I was a little protective.

ALEX: Apology accepted, Anuh-banana.

ANA laughs and abruptly stops.

ANA: Please don't.

ROB: Where is Will?

JEN: He just texted me. He should be here any minute.

ANA: Rob, I want you to know that I read this Tarzan book. Cover to cover… for you.

ROB: Ana, thank you.

JEN: I read it too.

LILY: Me too.

ALEX: So did I.

ROB: Wow. You read it? All of it? I'm amazed… all of you read it. The first book made such an impact on me. So… what… did you think!

WILL enters in his Brooks Brothers suit. He looks the same and yet… .

ANA: Oh Will–how are you?

WILL: I'm a completely changed man, Ana. And better than ever. Thank you for asking,

ANA: I'm sorry I didn't join you all for lunch. I just was… I was trying to write.

WILL: We missed you. But it was a great lunch.

ALEX: Delicious.

ANA: Alex, you went too?

ALEX: I did.

ROB: After, we took Will shopping to places I never knew existed.

WILL: Me neither.

LILY: The Pleasure Chest. Egor's Dungeon, Good Vibrations.

ANA: Oh, my.

WILL: Lily was the one that knew where they were.

ALEX: Lily knows everything.

LILY: Not everything, not yet.

WILL: It was wonderful. *(Pulls out a necklace out from under his button-down shirt.)* But I just bought this rainbow necklace.

ANA: Oh.

WILL: Can I tell you, my beloved Book Club… how it feels to turn the page and start a whole new chapter in my life?

ROB: How does it feel?

WILL: Liberating! There is a whole world out there… waiting for you… if you just go and look for it.

JEN: And then Will's parents came into town and joined us for dinner.

ANA: Oh. Lunch. Shopping. And dinner?

LILY: Your mom is so funny.

WILL: She loves to laugh.

JEN: Omigod, Mr. Nothnagel was so… emotional.

ANA: It must be a little difficult for your father to comes to terms with–

ALEX: "The day you know who you truly are is the day you become a true man."

WILL: That's my pops.

LILY: It was so sweet.

ROB: I wish my parents were half as… connected… to me.

WILL: My parents love you.

ROB: Thanks.

WILL: You are my brother, Rob.

ROB: You're my bro too.

JEN & LILY: Aww! Bromance!

WILL: I don't know how I would have survived all these years without your straight-forward honesty and your friendship.

ROB: Thanks, bro.

WILL: And can I tell you? No matter how hard, you should always tell the truth. It will set you free and lead you to happiness.

ROB: *(Beat. Maybe ROB strongly hugs WILL in appreciation and confesses.)* I didn't read *Return of Tarzan.* I'm sorry. I couldn't get through it.

ANA: Rob, you didn't read the book you picked?

ROB: Tarzan was nothing like I remembered. I guess I'm not fifteen years old anymore!

ANA: You didn't read *Return of Tarzan*?

ROB: No, honey.

ANA: Rob!

ROB: And there's something else, Ana.

ANA: What?

ROB: I turned down the promotion.

ANA: You turned down the vice president promotion? Why?

ROB: Being a V.P. is not who I want to be… at all.

ANA: Rob?

ROB: And Ana: I kissed Jen.

ANA: WHAT?!!!

JEN: Oh God.

ROB: I kissed Jen.

LILY: Whoa.

WILL: Um, buddy.

ANA: You kissed Jen?

ALEX: Oh boy.

ANA: What? When?

ROB: During Book Club… After *The Age of Innocence*.

ANA: During my Book Club. How?

ROB: I just leaned over… and kissed her.

ALEX: On the lips?

ANA: Alex! What are you doing in this conversation?

ROB: I kissed her. On the lips.

JEN: Ana, it was… nothing!

ANA: Jen. What is it with you and married men!

ROB: This is not Jen's fault.

ANA: I am your wife, Rob.

ROB: I was confused, and Jen is a good friend… but this happened because of us.

ANA: So this is our fault?

ROB: No. It's mine. I've done what was expected of me because it was easier than figuring out what I wanted. I want the flower of life. I want to grow. I want to try new things. And I think you do too. Ana, my "Age of Innocence" is over.

ANA: Oh my God. That friggin' book…

ROB: Ana, I'm sorry.

ANA: Sorry?! Sorry?! You read one book for Book Club and you're confused? Rob, you are my husband who kissed my friend Jen. Jen, you kissed my husband and brought that idiot into my Book Club. Will, my first love, you decide to re-write our entire history. And you all did it in my Book Club at my house! On camera! In front of everybody! Have you no sense? Have you no respect? Have you no manners? Lily, you are the only true blue person here.

LILY: Ana, I need to tell you something. The *Herald* wants to attract a younger, hipper, more *urbane* audience. Ana, they offered me the Friday column.

ANA: My Friday column? You are taking over my Connections column?

LILY: I wanted you to hear it from me… Ana, I'm so sorry.

ANA: You don't even like paper, you talented, little freak.

LILY: It's not personal.

ANA: It's personal to me! *(Stunned.)* You are my Book Club.

ROB: Ana—are you… OK?

ANA: Jesus H. Christ! No, Rob! I'm not OK! What is wrong with you people! Turn off that camera!

JEN: Ana, we can't!

ANA: Take it down! Take it down! Oh God. This is too much! Nobody can see this!

WILL: We can't stop the camera.

ANA: Cover it! Cover it!

ANA grabs a blanket and throws it over the camera. The stage goes dark for a couple of seconds. In the dark:

ANA: *(Cont'd.)* Arghh! I want to smash that machine!!

JEN: Ana, no!

WILL: Not the vase!

ANA: Lars, you've ruined my life. You've ruined my Book Club.

ROB: Ana!

LILY: Careful!

ANA: Lars, I hate you, I hate your film.

ANA yells, out of control.

ALL: Ana!

Lights back on: ALEX is holding the blanket that was covering the camera. The room is in disarray. WILL, LILY, JEN and ROB are all holding ANA. ALEX sits and watches.

ANA: Oh sweet Jesus! This is not the way Book Club is supposed to be!!!

WILL: Ana, you have to promise you will calm down.

ANA: I promise.

ROB: You have to control yourself.

ALEX: Book Club is like *Lord of the Flies* with wine and dip.

ANA: I am Ana Smith. I am Ana Smith. I'm… OK. I am always in control.

They let go of her. She's sniffling, but getting herself together. She looks around at everyone.

ANA: *(Cont'd.)* I have something I want to show you.

She walks out of the room and comes back holding a manuscript.

ANA: *(Cont'd.)* This is my book. My first three chapters.

ROB: You are writing a book?

WILL: About what?

ANA: All of you, even that jerk over there *(points to ALEX)* … have become more than my family, you have become a part of me. And this is my beautiful homage to what we had. *(Ceremoniously places the manuscript on the table.)* But I can't finish it… because the people I love and thought I knew… I don't know you anymore.

ROB: Ana, wait!

ANA exits. Everyone is stunned… ALEX goes up to the manuscript and picks it up.

ALEX: Ana's book is called *The Book Club.*

JEN: *The Book Club*?

ALEX: Ana has written a book… about all of us.

LILY: What!? No!

JEN: She can't do that!

WILL: She wouldn't!

ROB: She did.

LILY: *(Beat.)* What should we do?

ALEX: We should read it.

JEN: No!

ROB: I'm not sure that's what Ana wants us to do.

WILL: For once, I don't know if even Ana knows what Ana wants.

JEN: What is the worst thing reading this book could do?

LILY: *(Pause.)* I'll go get photocopies.

ALEX: Lily?

LILY: Yes?

ALEX: I can't wait to read your column.

LILY: Thank you, Alex. *(Exits.)*

JEN: We should buy pizza and wine.

WILL: Let's go. I'll drive.

ROB: Don't worry. We will be right back!

ROB, JEN and WILL exit.

ALEX watches them leave, then looks at the camera.

ALEX: Who the hell are these people? And why do I like them so much?

Lights shift.

Projection: **Mrs. Edith P. Simpson, Retired Librarian, High Point, North Carolina**.

Spotlight on EDITH (played by PUNDIT or LILY.) Wind is blowing. She is wearing goggles and a helmet and is about to jump out of a plane.

MRS. SIMPSON: I am Mrs. Simpson. And today I am thrilled to be learning to skydive.

Old Librarians can be crazy that way.

I am delighted to give you chickadees two little bits of advice.

One: read books. Real books. Books you can hold in your hand and carry in your head and your heart. My life has been decorated by every one of my foster kids and by every book I've ever read. In fact, yesterday, after sixty-two years of trying, I finally finished reading *Ulysses* by James Joyce.

Which brings me to my second bit of advice which is this: Get off your ass and do something with what you read. Because reading about life is not the same as living your life. Not the same at all. WHEEEEE! *(Jumps.)*

Projection: *The Book Club* by Ana Smith.

Everybody is reading in different positions. Pizza boxes, wine and paper plates are everywhere.

WILL: Unbelievable!

WILL is done with his book. He is stunned. He puts the manuscript on the table.

JEN: Good God Jupiter. Are you done already?

WILL: Yes. I'm done.

ROB: Well.

WILL: Keep reading.

Everybody dives back in. WILL takes a drink.

LILY gasps then laughs.

LILY: Oh no she did not.

JEN paces as she flips pages.

ROB: What?

LILY: Keep reading.

JEN: Oh my God. Oh my God!

ROB: Are you done?

JEN: OH MY GOD!

WILL: Have some wine.

LILY: All of that? In just three chapters?

ROB: OH! OH! OH!

He reads through the climax to the last sentence. He closes the book and throws the book down.

WILL: I know. Right?

Everyone is done except ALEX. They all wait for him. ALEX calmly turns the last page.

WILL: Alex?

ALEX: Done.

WILL: So?

ROB: Wow. That was intense.

JEN: I don't know what to say–

LILY: It's terrible and untrue.

ROB: Not all of it.

WILL: Enough of it.

WILL: She never told us she was writing about us!

JEN: She used our Book Club!

LILY: Everything we did and said in Book Club is in here!

JEN: It's amazing. And terrible.

LILY: It's like it's me… but it's not me. I know I said these things, but is that really who I am? I'm confused.

ROB: Me too! I don't know what to think.

ALEX: One thing is for sure: This book is going to sell! It is so… Ana. Smart and driven. Earnestly writing about friendship and food and books.

JEN: But our Book Club isn't really like this.

ANA opens the door.

ANA: Oh. I didn't think you all would still be here.

ROB: Are you all right, honey?

ANA: Of course I am, Rob. What a mess.

JEN: I'll say. Hi, Ana.

ANA: I'm sorry everything got so… uncomfortably intense.

ROB: Are you feeling better now?

ANA: I don't know.

WILL: Why don't you sit down?

WILL rights an overturned chair for her. She sits.

LILY: Ana, we read your book.

ANA: Oh! You did?

ALEX: We all did.

JEN: Yup, sure did.

ANA: It's only the first three chapters.

WILL: It's more than enough.

ANA: Oh. Thank you. It wasn't easy to write.

ROB: It wasn't easy to read, honey.

ALEX: Oh, I disagree. This is fun!

> "Ann's beautiful green eyes swept the room. Truth be
> known, in her lesser moments, Ann would selfishly dream
> of running away and releasing herself from the burden of
> her friends' unfulfilled lives. But she never would abandon
> her Book Club… "

ANA: Writing a book is harder than I thought. I've poured my
heart and soul into this.

LILY: Why didn't you tell us you were writing a book about
our Book Club?

ANA: It's really not so much about you all.

JEN: "Ann's heart burned with compassion for Jan. Poor Jan
was a woman of *promise* who had been eroded by her
predatory 'hussy' tendencies. She could have been a judge
or an astronaut, but instead, Jan had flittered her life away,
shuffling other people's papers and dreaming of tasting the
lips of men who would never love her."

ANA: In so many ways, Jan is the heroine of the story.

LILY: "Ann's gaze fell upon beautiful and vibrant Lula. It was
clear the smarmy professor Alvin was smitten with Lula.
He was a dangerous, vulgar man. Lula was utterly alone;
her mother had long vanished into the sepulchral haze of
crack cocaine. Ann knew she would have to mother where
another had failed.

ANA: Lily, you are a writer and editor. You realize this is a rough rough first draft.

WILL: "She could not help but wonder if she had chosen rightly. Would Phil not have been the perfect husband? The most devoted father? Phil's furtive looks her way filled her with despair. That the love had never died was undeniable… and yet… despite his nobility, there was something decidedly frumpy about Phil.

ROB: "And there was Bob. A college football quarterback, who had tackled Ann's senses with his sweet smile and steely abs. Ann knew Bob was a man with the soul of a poet trapped in the body of an all-American. Ann knew in her heart that he would always be there for her, even if he wasn't there for himself."

ANA: Ann loves Bob so much.

ROB: My name isn't Bob. And my abs are not so steely.

JEN: Ana! You can't just invent things about us.

WILL: Frumpy Phil is not me! In or out of the closet!

ANA: Guys! Guys!

LILY: I'm not a poor girl from the ghetto. My parents are dentists!

JEN: We're people, Ana. Not characters.

ANA: This is fiction, people! It's called literary license. You are my friends and you inspired these characters. You are complex and interesting people in my living room, but the truth is you are not compelling enough to be characters in a book. That's all.

ALEX: Ana is right. A potboiler must boil over.

ANA: I didn't mean to hurt any of you. It's just a book. These are just characters...

ALEX: "Just characters"? Think of it! There are billions of human beings that have passed through this earth, and the ones we remember the best, the ones that last: Scarlett O'Hara, Jane Eyre, Don Quixote, Heathcliff, well... they never existed. We live and we die and the matter of our daily lives evaporates the moment it happens. Except a part of us will live on, every time someone reads this book.

LILY: Ana, how does *The Book Club*–no–how does your book end? What happens to the rest of us? I mean them.

ANA: Well, I think Lula, she rises too quickly in her job... and finds herself successful but very alone.

LILY: Oh hell, no! It's not fair for Lula to be lonely for that long.

JEN: And what happens to Jan?

ROB: And Bob?

WILL: And Phil?

ALEX: Ana, what happens to the character of Ann?

ANA: I don't know. I'm stuck. And so are they. Those characters aren't developing into who I thought they would be. You know. This is all Lars Knudsen's fault. That bug-eyed camera changed everything. It made us self-conscious and intensely uncomfortable. Everyone, let's walk out right now, away from the judgmental eye of the camera, and continue our meeting at Starbucks. I'm sorry Lars Knudsen, but I must protect my Book Club.

WILL: It's *our* Book Club, Ana. OUR Book Club. And it was MY idea to start it!

ANA: OK! OK! It was your idea.

JEN: We are Book Club. We are a group!

ANA: Yes, and I am the glue of this group.

JEN: Ana, you are an amazing and strong woman. People like you run the world from PTAs to Congress. The world needs people like you.

ANA: Thank you, Jen.

JEN: But sometimes, people like you break things and you don't know it. You used our Book Club without our permission. Book Club is not ours anymore… it's just you. Ana… our Book Club is broken.

ANA: Book Club is broken?

WILL: Ana, our Book Club is done.

ANA absorbs the painful news.

ANA: My book broke Book Club?

ROB: *(Beat.)* Yes it did, honey.

ANA: Oh—Now I know what happens to the character of Ann: she loses everything.

ROB: *(Earnest.)* That's beautiful and tragic, honey.

ANA: *(Sinks to the floor.)* It's times like this when it really sucks being an overachiever. Who needs Book Club? Who needs to be social? Hell, who needs the inconvenience of having living breathing people in their living room? Well … I do. I need you. I love you.

She cries and falls apart.

ANA: *(Cont'd.)* Please forgive me. I never thought my book would hurt you. I'm so sorry. *(To ROB but it's too painful.)*

What am I going to do without you? Without my Book Club?

Beat. WILL picks up the manuscript.

WILL: Ana, you still have *your* Book Club.

LILY: Ana—You really should finish writing your book.

ANA: Really?

JEN: Yes, it was a painful, but a really good read.

ANA: Oh I would if I could… *(Beat.)* But… how should I end it all for these people? Sorry. These characters.

ALEX: *(Hands it to her.)* Any way you want, Ana. You are the author.

ANA: Right…

ALEX: You're in charge. You're in total control.

ANA: *(Beat.)* You're right. *(Beat.)* I'm the author. I'm in charge. *(Tentative.)* And in total control of this Book Club. Thank you, Alex! Beloved Book Club, I so appreciate your encouragement. I will go to Starbucks to write my Book Club book right now. *(Beat.)* You know, Rob, honey, I know it ruined everything… and I know it wasn't fun for you, but thank you for reading my book.

ROB walks up to her.

ROB: Ana, you are most complicated and infuriating woman I know.

He kisses her passionately.

ROB: *(Cont'd.)* You are the flower of my life.

ANA: Rob. Wow.

ROB: We have a lot to talk about. But now go write your book at Starbucks.

ANA: Thank you, honey. I really want to write this book. And then I have to get it published. And then, if I am lucky, I can sell the rights to make it into a movie.

ROB: A movie!!

ANA: Or a play.

Everyone looks at each other less enthused about the play idea.

ROB: Now is the right time, Ana.

ANA: *(Kisses him.)* Rob, you are my Tarzan, always. *(To all.)* Everyone, please clean up before I come back.

ANA leaves.

LILY: Alex, would you like to go to the opera or a poetry slam with me sometime?

ALEX: Lily, I would like that very much, thank you.

JEN: Will, will you have a baby with me?

WILL: What?

JEN: I don't want to interfere with your new life but would you father a child for me?

WILL: *(Delighted.)* Kids?! With me?

ROB: You'd be great parents.

WILL: A little Nothnagel in the world? Me? A pop? My parents will be so shocked. I would be honored, Jenny.

JEN: Thank you, Will.

ROB: I can't believe Book Club is breaking up.

LILY: I know, I am going to miss you all.

WILL: Me too. I am truly going to miss Book Club.

ALEX: What if one of YOU starts a new Book Club?

JEN: I can lead Book Club! Totally!

LILY: It can be a potluck!

JEN & LILY: Yes!

WILL: Oh! Can I join?

JEN: Of course!

ROB: I would like to come too.

WILL: Rob, really?!

ROB: Book Club is good for me.

JEN: Awesome!

ALEX: Can I come?

JEN: Yes, Alex.

ALEX: Awesome times two!

LILY: So this is our new Book Club!!!

ROB: Could I pick the book?

ALL: Yes.

ROB: I'm ready for something… epic. Where characters love and lose and grow. I want to travel to a land I've never seen and get to know people I've never met… and then feel at the end, that they are a part of me and my life

JEN: Yeah!

ALEX: Oh. We should read *War and Peace*.

LILY: Alex, That's an inspired choice.

ROB: Yeah! Let's read *War and Peace.*

WILL: All right, buddy!

LILY: Rob, I think it's more than a thousand pages.

JEN: Really? A thousand pages.

ROB: Oh… perfect!!

Lights out.

Epilogue. Lights up on:

ANA: My book *The Book Club* is a huge bestseller that's being made into a film by Martin Scorsese. More importantly, Rob and I are taking a really big new step by adopting a beautiful baby…

ROB: Gorilla… that lives in a wildlife preserve in Kenya! After reading *Wuthering Heights*, I totally want to call him Heathcliff!

WILL: You know, I read Dan Brown's other books and I did not like them. *The Da Vinci Code*, well… it was the right book at the right time. Some books just turn you upside down… and suddenly you can see the world right side up.

JEN: Will is a wonderful father to our two twin girls, Charlotte and Emily, and is dating a former Secret Service agent who loves Ernest Hemingway. I've gone back to law school! And I'm in the top of my class! And I still lose my keys all the time.

LILY: Book Club has been really good for me. Losing myself in a good book is like taking a journey. And finding someone who has read the same book is like finding a true soulmate on a lonely road.

ALEX: I got tenure at the university and celebrated by getting down on one knee and proposing.

LILY: I said, "Yes."

ALEX: God, *(looks at LILY)* I love… Book Club!

All actors take a bow and exit.

***Projection:* IN MEMORIAM**

Beat.

***Projection:* Edith P. Simpson, Librarian,**

Beat.

***Projection:* Sky-Diving Casualty**

The following list is aslo projected:

The Book Club Reading List (Books Cited):
Moby Dick; or, the Whale
Sounder
Old Yeller
Tarzan of the Apes
The Little House
Wuthering Heights
Paradise Lost
The Age of Innocence
Love in the Time of Cholera
Black Like Me
Native Son
The Color Purple
Beloved
Devil in a Blue Dress
Twilight
Fifty Shades of Grey
Ulysses
Search for Love
The Da Vinci Code
The Hunger Games
Harry Potter

Chicken Soup for the Soul
Lolita
Return of Tarzan
Charlotte's Web
Lord of the Flies
Gone With The Wind
Jane Eyre
Don Quixote of la Mancha
War and Peace
and
The Book Club
By Ana Smith
(A *New York Times* Bestseller)

DESTINY OF DESIRE

An Unapologetic Telenovela
in Two Acts

Destiny Of Desire was Originally Commissioned and Produced
by Arena Stage, Washington, DC

Molly Smith, Artistic Director

Edgar Dobie, Executive Producer

"From the first it has been the theatre's business to entertain people, as it also has of all the other arts. It is this business which always gives it its particular dignity; it needs no other passport than fun, but this it's got to have. We should not in any way be giving it a higher status if we were to turn it, e.g., into a purveyor of morality; it would on the contrary run the risk of becoming debased, and this would occur just as soon as it failed to make its moral lesson enjoyable, and enjoyable to the senses at that

a principle, admittedly, by which morality can only gain. Not even instruction can be demanded of it; at any rate, no more utilitarian lesson than how to move pleasurably, whether in the physical or in the spiritual sphere. The theatre must in short, remain something entirely superfluous, though this also means that it is the superfluous for which we live. Nothing needs less justification than pleasures."

--Bertolt Brecht
A Short Organum For The Theatre (1948)

DESTINY OF DESIRE
By Karen Zacarías
An Unapologetic Telenovela in Two Acts

First Choice: AN ALL LATINO CAST
Second Choice: A very diverse cast

NOTES: The ten ACTORS (five women/five men) and hopefully one (or more) musicians enter and hang out or sit in chairs around the playing arena. The actors are both the ENSEMBLE ACTORS that employ Brechtian techniques of: Quotes and Titles and Songs. And they are the CHARACTERS of *Destiny of Desire*.

The actors' individual back story is not important...but how we see them collectively supporting the action in the playing arena is vital. They construct the story. Once they enter as characters of *Destiny of Desire*: they are always truthful, committed, and in the moment when in a scene. We can see them watch on the sidelines as the action unfolds.

No camp. No fake Spanish accents (real ones are fine). DELIVERY should be Intense and Sharp and Clear with Great Pacing. Think on the Line. Communicating without explaining. Heightened but centered.

In my mind: *Destiny of Desire* is Beautiful Extravagant Poor Theater. There is a heightened theatricality to the story; it is a delicious populist Greek tragedy, but it is still grounded in the humanity of joy and suffering, and steeped in the culture and community that creates it and celebrates it.

The Brechtian quotes must be current national facts that (progressively) contextualize the issue in the scene. If the play is performed in the U.S., the facts must be about the U.S. If performed in Mexico or Bulgaria...the facts must correspond to the country of performance. FYI: Sources for the current quotes are at the end of this script.

Setting: An abandoned theater in (*hometown*).

ACT I

Scene 1: Life, Death And Destiny

Scene 2: A Chance Encounter

Scene 3: Betrayal And Unexpected Outcome

Scene 4: Mothers And Daughters

Scene 5: Secrets And Lies

Scene 6: More Secrets And Lies

Scene 7: Servants, Poets…Sisters?

Scene 8: Taking A Chance On Love

Scene 9: A Surprising Turn Of Events

A BREAK IN THE ACTION

ACT II

Scene 1: Sorrow And Loss

Scene 2: Regrets Over Drinks

Scene 3: Another Surprising Turn of Events

Scene 4: Climax

Scene 5: Servants, Poets, And Daughters

Scene 6: Life, Destiny, And Denouement

Characters

HORTENCIA DEL RIO – (age 35-45) A poor mother who due to circumstances becomes a maid to the richest woman in town.

ERNESTO DEL RIO – (age 35-45) Her hardworking poor husband. A farmer.

VICTORIA MARIA DEL RIO-NURSE 1 – (age 18) Their beautiful yet sickly daughter.

ARMANDO CASTILLO – (age 50-70) Owner of the Castillo Casino. The most powerful and richest man in town.

FABIOLA CASTILLO – (age 35-45) The beauty queen wife of Armando Castillo.

PILAR ESPERANZA CASTILLO/NURSE 2 – (age 18) Their beautiful daughter.

SEBASTIÁN JOSE CASTILLO/PARAMEDIC 1 – (age 37) ARMANDO's estranged son from a former marriage.

DOCTOR JORGE RAMIRO MENDOZA/CASINO DEALER/COP – (Age 45-60) The Head of the hospital.

DR. DIEGO MENDOZA/PARAMEDIC 2/COP 2 – (age 30-35) His kind and handsome estranged son, also a doctor.

SISTER SONIA – (age 50-60) A nurse who is a nun.

SISTER SONIA

    Turn off your phones.

    Photos are prohibited.

    Locate your nearest emergency exit.

    You are our live audience...so...be alive!

    Unwrap your candy whenever you want.

Act I

SCENE 1: LIFE, DEATH AND DESTINY

Prologue. ACTORS come in and discover an abandoned theater. They pull off cloth to find a piano and arrange chairs. We see them warm up get dressed.

ALL: 'Destiny of Desire – An Unapologetic Telenovela: in Two Acts'. We are here to change the social order. Deal with it.

SISTER SONIA: It is a rainy and stormy night...

The actors take the cue immediately and start to create the sound of wind and rain...it might then be overtaken by the real sounds of rain. Or real rain.

... here...at the hospital

Hospital sounds. A woman puts a rolled up blanket under her shirt. A man decides to hold her hand. They walk on stage. ERNESTO and HORTENCIA enter.

ACTOR (ARMANDO): (With placard:) Life, death and destiny.

ERNESTO: Please–we need your help.

SISTER SONIA: Oh dear goodness.

HORTENCIA: The baby–is coming–

SISTER SONIA: You are trembling with cold.

More rain. Lightning.

ERNESTO: We walked on the desert road in the rain.

HORTENCIA: Oh–that hurts.

ERNESTO: Her water broke a mile back.

SISTER SONIA: I am Sister Sonia.

HORTENCIA: Hortencia del Rio.

ERNESTO: Ernesto del Rio. We live on a farm on the outskirts of town.

HORTENCIA: I must lie down.

Hortencia moans.

ERNESTO: Please–she needs a doctor. Help us!

SISTER SONIA: I will get Dr. Mendoza immediately.

Suddenly a very rich FABIOLA rushes (in a gurney)–immediately DOCTOR MENDOZA, and NURSE 1 are at her side. FABIOLA is also in full labor.

FABIOLA: Help me–Help me! Doctor Mendoza. My child arrives!

DOCTOR MENDOZA: Señora Castillo! I am here for you.

NURSE 1 runs on, also a novice.

SISTER SONIA: That is Fabiola Castillo–the beauty queen wife of Armando Castillo–

ERNESTO: Owner of the Castillo Casino.

FABIOLA is wheeled around the stage. She moves her hands in pain, but it eerily looks like a pained beauty queen waving from a float. FABIOLA screams.

NURSE 1: Her blood pressure is dropping.

DR. MENDOZA: Sister Sonia. I need you with this patient.

DOCTOR MENDOZA moves with FABIOLA to a private room and his entourage.

HORTENCIA: *(Moans. Lies on the floor.)* Oh please. Why is this so painful?

ERNESTO: What is wrong?

SISTER SONIA: Nothing is wrong. The baby is coming. Nurse!

NURSE 2 enters, a young novice.

NURSE 2: Yes, sister?

SISTER SONIA: Help me deliver this baby.

NURSE 2: Here? On the dirty floor? With no doctor?

SISTER SONIA: We have no alternative.

On the other side of the stage: in the private room with FABIOLA.

FABIOLA: Why is my chest in so much pain?

DOCTOR MENDOZA: The mother's heart is beating erratically.

NURSE 1: The baby is coming.

DOCTOR MENDOZA: Push!

SIMULTANEOUSLY both HORTENCIA and FABIOLA start to give birth.

SISTER SONIA: Push!

FABIOLA AND HORTENCIA: I am pushing–

NURSE 1: We are losing power.

ERNESTO: The storm is so strong!

The storm is raging; the lights at the hospital flicker.

Lightning. The lights go out.

SISTER SONIA: We lost power.

Quiet. We hear the cry of two babies being born. Generator lights come on.

SISTER SONIA is holding a large rolled-up blanket. Dr. Mendoza holds up a delicate pink rolled up dress or blanket.

DOCTOR MENDOZA: A girl!

SISTER SONIA: A beautiful baby girl.

HORTENCIA AND FABIOLA: A girl!

ERNESTO: You did it.

HORTENCIA: We did it.

FABIOLA: I DID IT!

FABIOLA faints.

SISTER SONIA: Doctor Mendoza must examine the baby.

ERNESTO and HORTENCIA rest. SISTER SONIA and NURSE 2, who is holding the baby, come into FABIOLA's room. The DOCTOR is reviving FABIOLA. NURSE 1 holds FABIOLA's sickly baby.

DOCTOR MENDOZA: Her heart stopped! Oh no!

SISTER SONIA: Oh no–

NURSE 1 AND NURSE 2: No!

DOCTOR MENDOZA: Armando Castillo will have my head if she dies.

DOCTOR MENDOZA hits FABIOLA's chest. He listens and finds a heartbeat.

Her heart beats once more.

Beat.

NURSE 1: It was a very difficult birth.

SISTER SONIA: How is her baby?

NURSE 1 shows it to her.

God have mercy on her soul. She is so tiny and frail.

DOCTOR MENDOZA: Poor thing. The child will not survive for long.

SISTER SONIA: And the mother? Will she live?

DOCTOR MENDOZA: Nurse, call Armando Castillo. He should see his wife and child before they both before… before–

FABIOLA: Before…what?

Underscoring. Everybody pivots and looks at FABIOLA who is awake.

DOCTOR MENDOZA: Señora Castillo–

FABIOLA: Who dares send for my husband? You wish for him to see me like this? Dripping with sweat and blood?

She cries for a moment and then gets angry. She tears off the sheets.

NO! Get me clean sheets. Immediately. And make sure they are soft and fresh. Go!

NURSE 2 gives the baby to SISTER SONIA and runs out.

DOCTOR MENDOZA: Señora, you must calm down.

FABIOLA: Where is my baby?

HORTENCIA: Where is my baby?

DOCTOR MENDOZA: Be careful Señora–you have lost a lot of blood.

FABIOLA: I am fine.

ERNESTO: I am sure she is fine.

FABIOLA: A daughter is what Armando wanted–and I delivered! Let me see my baby!

NURSE 2 hands baby to her.

Nurse, now call for my husband.

NURSE 2 exits.

(Really looking at her baby.) She is so very small.

DOCTOR MENDOZA: Señora, your daughter's heart is weak.

FABIOLA: No. Not weak.

DOCTOR MENDOZA: And you will die if you have another child.

ERNESTO: We will cherish her.

SISTER SONIA: You must cherish her.

FABIOLA: Stop: My daughter must be strong. She must be beautiful.

DOCTOR MENDOZA: Señora Castillo–I see this is difficult to understand.

FABIOLA: I cannot bring home a child that is broken and tell my husband that she is all he can expect from me. Armando Castillo does not like to be disappointed.

SISTER SONIA: Rumor has it that Armando Castillo killed his first wife.

DOCTOR MENDOZA: Sister Sonia! It was a terrible boating accident. Armando and the police never found her body. He was devastated.

FABIOLA: Until he met me. This child will destroy our marriage. She brings me only despair.

HORTENCIA: I am so happy. And so nervous.

ERNESTO: Me too. I love you, Hortencia.

HORTENCIA: And I love you.

They kiss.

FABIOLA: Sister… Is that another baby in your arms…?!

SISTER SONIA: This is Hortencia del Rio's baby. She is married to a farmer–

FABIOLA: Is the baby a girl?

SISTER SONIA: Yes.

FABIOLA: And she is a strong healthy child?

SISTER SONIA: Yes.

FABIOLA: I want that baby.

SISTER SONIA: No.

FABIOLA: My sickly child will die. And the healthy child in your arms will live the meaningless life of a peasant. But I could change her fate.

*ACTOR *(PILAR)*: At hospitals in the United States, about 1 in 8 babies is given to the wrong mother. Temporarily or permanently.

HORTENCIA: What shall we name our daughter?

ERNESTO: We will name her after your mother.

SISTER SONIA: What about her mother? She gave birth to a healthy child.

DOCTOR MENDOZA: An unexpected complication arose… and her baby became sick.

SISTER SONIA: Doctor Mendoza, what are you saying?

FABIOLA: The poor expect to suffer. That is their fate.

DOCTOR MENDOZA: And that woman will be pregnant again by next week.

FABIOLA: And I will be barren, baby-less, and abandoned by my husband.

SISTER SONIA: We all have our cross to bear.

FABIOLA: I will give that little girl everything she wants!

HORTENCIA: I hope we can give her everything she needs.

FABIOLA: I will employ her mother as my nanny, she will help raise her daughter.

HORTENCIA: I will work day and night to make sure her dreams are fulfilled.

ERNESTO: So will I. We can do this.

SISTER SONIA: You cannot do this!

DOCTOR MENDOZA: Sister, enough!

FABIOLIA: Sister Sonia–how dare you judge me? You do not have a husband. You do not have a family.

SISTER SONIA: The convent is my family. I was a lost soul until the nuns took me in.

FABIOLA: When my father's fortune burned to the ground, I lost everything. Now, I am the wife of the wealthiest man in Bellarica. The Lord helps those that help themselves.

NURSES run in.

NURSE 2: Señor Castillos's limousine just pulled up.

NURSE 1: Here–the new sheets…soft and fresh just as you requested.

FABIOLA: Pull up my hair–Add some color. Now go greet Señor Castillo.

NURSES exit.

How do I look?

Maybe an ACTOR focuses a warm light on FABIOLA.

DOCTOR MENDOZA: You are glowing.

FABIOLA: Pain makes me beautiful.

HORTENCIA: You make me feel beautiful.

FABIOLA: Now, hand me my new baby.

DOCTOR MENDOZA comes to take the baby away from SISTER SONIA who resists.

DOCTOR MENDOZA: Sister, do not deny this baby this opportunity.

SISTER SONIA: *(Looking at the baby in her arms.)* Maybe that baby will have a better life.

SISTER SONIA hands the healthy baby to DOCTOR MENDOZA who hands it to FABIOLA.

FABIOLA: As the daughter of Armando Castillo, I assure you, she will.

SISTER SONIA takes the frail baby.

DOCTOR MENDOZA: You will see. We are doing the right thing.

SISTER SONIA: *(Holding the doomed child.)* Oh little one, you are too frail for this cruel world.

SISTER SONIA begins to exit. An actor puts on a tuxedo coat and becomes ARMANDO CASTILLO. He enters and runs into SISTER SONIA.

ARMANDO: I am Armando Castillo. Where is my wife?

SISTER SONIA: Resting in the emergency room.

ARMANDO: Emergency Room!

SISTER SONIA: Your wife had complications with her heart. But she is fine now. You have a daughter.

ARMANDO: Is this my baby? She looks so frail.

SISTER SONIA: This is the baby of another. The doctor says she will not live long.

ARMANDO: How terrible.

SISTER SONIA: But the baby... in your wife's arms is healthy and strong.

ARMANDO: A beautiful baby girl. Thank you sister.

ARMANDO enters FABIOLA's room.

DOCTOR MENDOZA: Señor Castillo!

ARMANDO: Fabiola, my queen.

FABIOLA: Armando, my king.

ARMANDO: The nun told me everything!

FABIOLA and DOCTOR MENDOZA look at each other in panic.

FABIOLA: Everything?

SISTER SONIA enters ERNESTO's and HORTENCIA's room.

SISTER SONIA: *(Clears her throat.)* Señor and Señora del Rio.

HORTENCIA: Sister, you were gone so long.

ERNESTO: We were worried.

SISTER SONIA: I did not forget you.

ERNESTO: We decided on a name.

HORTENCIA: Victoria Maria.

ERNESTO: Victoria Maria.

SISTER SONIA: What a beautiful name!

HORTENCIA: Can I hold her? She must be hungry.

SISTER SONIA hands her the baby.

Why is she so silent?

ERNESTO: What is wrong with our baby?

Back to FABIOLA's room.

DOCTOR MENDOZA: Sister Sonia told you–

FABIOLA: Everything?

ARMANDO: Yes.

Beat.

About your heart.

DOCTOR MENDOZA: *(Relief.)* Señora Castillo's heart is delicate.

FABIOLA: It was a medical hiccup, nothing!

ARMANDO: Nothing? Your heart is my heart, my love. Doctor, I will give you the money you require to buy the necessary cardiology equipment.

ARMANDO opens his check book and writes a check.

FABIOLA: I am strong. I am fine!

ARMANDO: I have been a widower once; I will not lose my precious Fabiola.

Writes a check gives it to DOCTOR MENDOZA.

Let me know if you need more.

DOCTOR MENDOZA: I certainly will. Thank you.

ARMANDO: So…is this my child?

Back to ERNESTO and HORTENCIA.

ERNESTO: Tell us, what is wrong with our baby?

SISTER SONIA: The Truth about your baby is–

(DOCTOR MENDOZA runs into ERNESTO's room still holding the check.)

DOCTOR MENDOZA: Your baby is very ill.

HORTENCIA: Doctor, what are you saying?

DOCTOR MENDOZA: I am afraid her death is imminent. God willing, you will have other children soon.

ERNESTO: Our Victoria Maria is our miracle from God.

HORTENCIA: There can be no others.

SISTER SONIA: I am so sorry.

DOCTOR MENDOZA: None of us can fight her destiny.

Back to ARMANDO and FABIOLA.

ARMANDO: So this is my child?

FABIOLA: Of course, my love. Here she is.

ARMANDO holds the baby.

ARMANDO: Wait. This baby, she looks nothing like me!

Turns and worried looks.

Back to ERNESTO and HORTENCIA.

HORTENCIA: Help my poor baby.

DOCTOR MENDOZA: I am afraid she has already stopped breathing.

HORTENCIA: No! She blinked at me but a second ago.

DOCTOR MENDOZA listens to her heart. He shakes his head.

DOCTOR MENDOZA: She is gone. I am sorry. Time of death. 4:00 am.

Hands her back the baby. HORTENCIA and ERNESTO are devastated and shocked.

SISTER SONIA: Hortencia. Save your child. Breathe into her.

ERNESTO: Breathe into her now!

HORTENCIA tries to breathes life into her baby.

DOCTOR MENDOZA: It will not work.

He is right. DOCTOR MENDOZA is satisfied and starts to exit.

I am so sorry.

SISTER SONIA: Wait! Listen!

We see ACTOR (VICTORIA) do a baby cry into the microphone off stage.

HORTENCIA: She lives!

ERNESTO: You have saved her life, Hortencia.

SISTER SONIA: It is a miracle from God.

Back to ARMANDO and FABIOLA.

ARMANDO: And I know why she looks nothing like me!

Turns and worried looks.

FABIOLA: *(Terrified.)* Why?

ARMANDO: Because she takes after her beautiful mother–
Thank God.

Back to ERNESTO and HORTENCIA.

ERNESTO: Thank God!

DOCTOR MENDOZA: Your baby has a weak heart that will
stop beating, very soon.

HORTENCIA: Help my baby. Help her live. There must be
something you can do!

DOCTOR MENDOZA:	SISTER SONIA:
No. There is not.	Yes, there is.

DOCTOR MENDOZA: Sister Sonia–

SISTER SONIA: Doctor Mendoza just received very generous
funds from…

DOCTOR MENDOZA: An anonymous donor…

SISTER SONIA: Doctor we could have a new neo-natal heart
unit delivered by tomorrow.

DOCTOR MENDOZA: It is no use!

HORTENCIA: Doctor Jorge Ramiro Mendoza. You are
the man, the only man, with the power, wisdom and
compassion to rescue her. Please save her. She needs you.
I need you.

DOCTOR MENDOZA: *(Ripple of music. Falls in love with her.
Beat.)* Señora del Rio. I vow to be by your side and help
you.

ERNESTO: Victoria is our baby.

ARMANDO: My baby.

FABIOLA: I always make sure Armando Castillo gets what he wants. She is my gift.

ERNESTO: She is our light.

ARMANDO: She is my legacy.

HORTENCIA: She is our life.

SISTER SONIA: This baby is blessed.

HORTENCIA: She is a blessing from God for us.

ARMANDO: This baby is the blood of my blood. The Castillo family fortune will be hers!

HORTENCIA: *(Holding her close.)* Victoria Maria del Rıo–

ARMANDO: *(Holding her up.)* Pilar Esperanza Josefina Castillo–

HORTENCIA AND ERNSESTO AND ARMANDO: …You are our Destiny.

A SONG OF DESTINY AND DESIRE (THE OPENING THEME SONG/CREDITS)

We see the opening credits song: a theatrical musical collage that suggests the conflicts of the story and the passage of eighteen years.

CHORUS
Montua/Chorus
> EL DESTINO DEL DESEO
> EL DESEO DEL DESTINO
> ME CONSUMEN COMO EL FUEGO
> Y TU AMOR ES EL CAMINO

> EL DESTINO DEL DESEO
> EL DESEO DEL DESTINO
> ME CONSUMEN COMO EL FUEGO
> Y TU AMOR ES EL CAMINO

Verse 1

DICEN QUE MI DESTINO
ESTÁ ESCRITO EN LAS ESTRELLAS
JURAN QUE LA FORTUNA
ESTÁ CALCADA EN MIS HUELLAS
QUE AL NACER MI SUERTE FUE
DECIDIDA CON UN DADO
QUE EN LA APUESTA DEL AMOR
YO SIEMPRE LLEVO LA MANO

Verse 2

Y ME ENTREGO POR ENTERO
AL ANDAR DE MI CAMINO
PORQUE LAS CARTAS ME DICEN
LO QUE ME TRAERÁ EL DESTINO
AUNQUE DIGAN QUE MI SINO
ESTÁ MARCADO EN MI FRENTE
YA SABRÁN QUE MI DESTINO
LO DECIDO CON MI MENTE

Pre-chorus

ROMPERÉ TODAS LAS REGLAS
APOSTARÉ CON MI SUERTE
GANARÉ TODOS LOS JUEGOS
HASTA EL DÍA DE MI MUERTE

Montuno/Chorus

EL DESTINO DEL DESEO
EL DESEO DEL DESTINO
ME CONSUMEN COMO EL FUEGO
Y TU AMOR ES EL CAMINO
EL DESTINO DEL DESEO
EL DESEO DEL DESTINO
ME CONSUMEN COMO EL FUEGO

Y TU AMOR ES EL CAMINO
EL DESTINO DEL DESEO
EL DESEO DEL DESTINO
ME CONSUMEN COMO EL FUEGO
Y TU AMOR ES EL CAMINO
EL DESTINO DEL DESEO
EL DESEO DEL DESTINO
ME CONSUMEN COMO EL FUEGO
Y TU AMOR ES EL CAMINO

SCENE 2: EIGHTEEN YEARS LATER: A CHANCE ENCOUNTER

The Park. Eighteen years later. Beautiful eighteen-year-old PILAR extends her baby blanket and sits on it.

ACTOR (DR. DIEGO): (With placard:) Eighteen years later. A chance encounter.

PILAR is talking on the phone. A stressful conversation.

PILAR: Mami, please, I do not wish to go to the ball. My priorities? I promise I will be home in time for the fitting. I love–she hung up on me.

Sighs.

Quiet and solitude. Finally.

A handsome thirty-six-year-old SEBASTIÁN bikes in. He has a briefcase. He's on his phone and talking.

SEBASTIÁN: We wait until we have 33% of the market shares before we even discuss the dividends. My analysis of the Dow predicted this correction in the market.

SEBASTIÁN trips over PILAR. He falls flat and his telephone flies out of his hand.

PILAR: Be careful.

SEBASTIÁN: That is a new phone.

They each crawl in different directions to get their stuff.

PILAR: My notebook!

SEBASTIÁN:	PILAR *(CONT'D)*:
Look at you.	Look at you.
Lying in people's way.	Wandering around without looking where you are going.

SEBASTIÁN and PILAR turn and finally do look at each other. A ripple of music. They stare. They continue to stare. They are immediately in love.

PILAR *(CONT'D)*: I beg your pardon. I do not know what came over me.

SEBASTIÁN: The apology is all mine...I/...I...I...

PILAR: /You...you...you

He hands her her book.

SEBASTIÁN: This...is yours? Your diary?

PILAR: No. My poetry.

SEBASTIÁN: These words are your poems?

PILAR: These words are my wings.

SEBASTIÁN: May I?

PILAR: No!

Beat.

Yes.

SEBASTIÁN: If only you knew...That the wind that whispers by your ear
Is my Desire

A butterfly born from the curve of my hips,
Rising with the heat of my breast
Fluttering toward the light.

SEBASTIÁN AND PILAR: Until she lands a delicate kiss
On the petals that are your lips.

SEBASTIÁN: Did you write this for your love?

PILAR: No. I have a very active imagination.

SEBASTIÁN: May I read another?

PILAR: *(Laughs.)* Not today.

She holds out her hand. He hands her the book.

What is your business here in the beautiful, prosperous
town of Bellarica?

SEBASTIÁN: I am here to meet with the head of the highest-
stakes casino in town.

PILAR: Are you meeting with Armando Castillo?

SEBASTIÁN: Of course, he owns the Castillo Casino.

PILAR: The Monaco of Mexico!

SEBASTIÁN: But his great casino has not changed with the
times. I have a plan involving online technology that will
generate new revenue streams for his casino.

PILAR: All you really need to gamble is greed. And this town
has plenty of that already.

SEBASTIÁN: Gambling is about hope; beating the odds to get
what you desire.

PILAR: And what people want is money.

SEBASTIÁN: People gamble for a chance at a better life.
People who walk into a casino will risk what they have for

something they desire: money, respect, or, if they are like me, love.

PILAR: *(Beat.)* Then let me give you some advice, when you play against the Castillo Casino, the house always wins.

SEBASTIÁN: Well, maybe not this time.

PILAR: Armando Castillo is a shrewd businessman. You should be careful.

SEBASTIÁN: Are you careful?

PILAR: Not when I allow a man I never met to touch my palm.

SEBASTIÁN: I feel…I feel like I know you.

PILAR: Yes. Like I have always known you.

SEBASTIÁN: I want to kiss you.

PILAR: I want you to kiss me too.

He leans in. She gets overwhelmed.

But not yet.

SEBASTIÁN: Then when?

PILAR: The next time we meet.

SEBASTIÁN: And when will that be?

PILAR: It might be in an hour. It might be in a day. It might be in a year. Our next meeting, I will be older and wiser than I am now. You must kiss me then.

SEBASTIÁN: I look forward to our next meeting.

PILAR: I must leave before I do something I might regret.

SEBASTIÁN: Wait! How can I reach you?

PILAR: I bet our paths will cross again.

SEBASTIÁN: I refuse to leave my fate up to chance.

PILAR: Well, Señor, perhaps you came to the wrong town.

PILAR scampers off to a seat with the chorus.

SEBASTIÁN: Wait! I do not even know your name!

*ACTOR *(ERNESTO)*: In the United States, chance encounters have a 25% higher rate of failure than online dating.

SCENE 3: BETRAYAL AND AN UNEXPECTED OUTCOME

The Farm. HORTENCIA's and ERNESTO's house. HORTENCIA is sewing. DOCTOR MENDOZA knocks.

*ACTOR *(VICTORIA MARIA): (With placard:)* Betrayal and an unexpected outcome.

HORTENCIA: Doctor, what are you doing here?

DOCTOR MENDOZA: I wanted to pay a home visit.

HORTENCIA: I am sorry you came all this way for nothing. Victoria felt well today and she left for school.

DOCTOR MENDOZA: I know. I saw Ernesto drive away with her.

HORTENCIA: Oh–

DOCTOR MENDOZA: Hortencia, I am here to see you.

HORTENCIA: Oh, is there another bill I need to pay? We no longer have health insurance–

DOCTOR MENDOZA: No. I am here for you.

HORTENCIA: Doctor Mendoza–please, not again.

DOCTOR MENDOZA: I love you. I was a lonely doctor with no purpose until I met you. I saved your daughter's life. And you saved mine. We can no longer deny our destiny.

HORTENCIA: I love my husband.

DOCTOR MENDOZA: He does not deserve you. He hardly sees you.

HORTENCIA: He works too much–with the farm, cutting old brush and all the odd jobs he can find. Our daughter needs a new heart.

DOCTOR MENDOZA: A new heart?

HORTENCIA: I have researched…at the Castillo House, there is a computer.

DOCTOR MENDOZA: A heart transplant is too risky. Victoria is not strong enough.

HORTENCIA: She is stronger than you and I both.

DOCTOR MENDOZA: If you really want to help your daughter, you should leave Ernesto. You will no longer have to scrub Fabiola Castillo's floors. I will look after Victoria's health on a daily basis. Hortencia, I want you to marry me.

HORTENCIA: Doctor you are already married!

DOCTOR MENDOZA: I will leave my wife for you.

HORTENCIA: No–not for me.

DOCTOR MENDOZA: I can have my lawyers deliver divorce papers today.

Beat.

The path is clear for you and I to do what in our hearts we both want. This.

He kisses her. She yields. Sweeping romantic music.

HORTENCIA: Doctor, this is not what I want.

The music stops. ERNESTO enters.

ERNESTO: Hortencia!

HORTENCIA: Ernesto!

ERNESTO: Dr. Mendoza!

DOCTOR MENDOZA: Ernesto! You are not supposed to be here.

ERNESTO: Today, I have to cut the scrub behind the school. So we turned back for this: my machete.

He holds up a machete.

What in the devil's name is going on here?

DOCTOR MENDOZA: Hortencia and I have been having an affair for eighteen years.

ERNESTO: Hortencia is this true?

HORTENCIA: He lies. Dr. Mendoza, leave!

DOCTOR MENDOZA: She is soft and wants to spare your feelings. But I am not scared to tell you the truth.

HORTENCIA: Ernesto!

ERNESTO drops the machete, and turns around without a weapon.

ERNESTO: The woman I love is neither a liar, nor a fool. I suggest you do what she says and get out immediately.

DOCTOR MENDOZA: And abandon the woman I love? Never.

HORTENCIA: I do not love you.

DOCTOR MENDOZA: You whispered something different in my arms last night.

ERNESTO: Get out! Now!

DOCTOR MENDOZA: Your daughter is alive thanks to me. Her delicate health still hangs in the balance.

ERNESTO: Do not threaten our daughter's life!

DOCTOR MENDOZA: I will do what I want!

DOCTOR MENDOZA punches ERNESTO. A fight ensues.

HORTENCIA: No, Dr. Mendoza…Ernesto…no.

There is a struggle… DOCTOR MENDOZA grabs the machete during the fight and is about to attack ERNESTO. Then: VICTORIA runs on with a gun. She points it squarely at DOCTOR MENDOZA's back.

VICTORIA: Stop! Turn around thief.

DOCTOR MENDOZA slowly does.

Doctor Mendoza?

*ACTOR *(SISTER SONIA): (We see her, off stage. Very loudly:)* Bang! Bang!

HORTENCIA: What happened?

VICTORIA: Oh, no! I must have accidentally pulled the trigger.

ERNESTO: The doctor has been shot!

DR. MENDOZA: Oh no.

HORTENCIA: In the chest!

ERNESTO: Oh no, he is collapsing.

DOCTOR MENDOZA collapses.

VICTORIA: I thought you were a bandit trying to steal from us. I only meant to scare you.

ERNESTO: Victoria will go to prison. We must save him.

HORTENCIA: Ernesto–call an ambulance.

He runs off.

Doctor, can you hear me? Say something please.

DOCTOR MENDOZA: *(Trying to get a kiss.)* Hortencia, you must breathe into me.

ERNESTO walks in.

HORTENCIA: There is no use. He has lost all consciousness!

DOCTOR MENDOZA surrenders to his coma.

VICTORIA: Is he dying? After all he has done to help me?

HORTENCIA: Daughter, give me the gun.

VICTORIA: No Mami. I committed the crime. I am the one that shot him.

HORTENCIA: You must never say that!

HORTENCIA grabs the gun from her daughter.

Ernesto, get her out of here! Take her as far away from here as you can.

VICTORIA: No, Mami.

ERNESTO: I will not leave you, Hortencia.

HORTENCIA: Dr. Mendoza is my lover. We were about to make love when you walked in.

ERNESTO: You are lying.

HORTENCIA: I have been his mistress for years.

ERNESTO: That cannot be true.

HORTENCIA: You never look at me anymore. If you did, you would see that the Doctor is the one I truly desire.

VICTORIA: Mami–

ERNESTO: I am sorry.

HORTENCIA: Now get Victoria out of here.

Light or sirens getting closer.

ERNESTO takes a crying VICTORIA out. HORTENCIA administers to DOCTOR MENDOZA.

VICTORIA starts to have trouble breathing. Her heart hurts. ERNESTO holds VICTORIA and calms her attack.

ERNESTO: Victoria, you must calm down. Remember your heart. Breathe. Slowly. Good.

VICTORIA: What is happening?

ERNESTO: If the doctor dies, you will get sicker and sicker! God help me!

He and VICTORIA exit. The paramedics enter and put DR. MENDOZA on the gurney.

*ACTOR *(PARAMEDIC/DR. DIEGO)*: Last year 285 children under the age of eighteen picked up a firearm and accidentally shot themselves or someone else.

HORTENCIA: Doctor Mendoza, you must live! Or I will spend the rest of my life locked away from the people I love most.

SCENE 4: MOTHERS AND DAUGHTERS

The Castillo mansion.

*ACTOR *(HORTENCIA)*: Mothers and daughters.

FABIOLA: Pilar! Pilar Esperanza! Show me your dress.

Maybe, we see PILAR finish dressing.

PILAR: Please. No. I want to stay home and write!

FABIOLA: No. You are going to the Castillo Charity Ball.

PILAR enters in a very vavoomy fancy dress.

PILAR: Wearing this?

FABIOLA: Listen to your…mother. The fate of a woman is always written by the hand of a man. And you are not getting any younger. Eat less. Show more leg.

PILAR: Papi cannot approve of this.

ARMANDO enters.

ARMANDO: Papi? What about Papi?

PILAR runs to him.

PILAR: Papi. Oh Papi.

ARMANDO: My princess.

PILAR: The ball…this dress.

ARMANDO: Let me see you. Fabiola, the color makes her skin look way too dark.

FABIOLA: I agree.

ARMANDO: Stay out of the sun, Pilar.

PILAR: What is wrong with my skin?

FABIOLA: Maybe if we lighten her hair.

ARMANDO: Strands of blonde would certainly better illuminate her class and upbringing.

FABIOLA: We should also shorten the dress.

ARMANDO: Class, Fabiola. Class! This is the Castillo Charity Ball.

FABIOLA: A rose dress. Elegant. Enticing. Regal.

ARMANDO: Yes. The perfect dress for the Castillo Charity Ball tomorrow. Pilar, you are a blossom at her prime. Now is the time to find you a husband from an elite family and secure your future.

PILAR: Papi, I am going to the University.

ARMANDO: No. The University is for the sniveling middle classes. And a waste of time for a pretty girl like you.

FABIOLA: The burden of beauty.

PILAR: But the creative writing department at the Public University is nationally recognized.

ARMANDO: Nothing but infectious radicals, and revolutionaries at the Public University.

PILAR: Exactly, I want to write poetry and to teach. I am first in my class. I have won awards for my poems.

FABIOLA: Wake up, child. Of course "you" won. Only a fool would deny a first place to the daughter of Armando Castillo.

PILAR: I sent them anonymously. And I still won.

ARMANDO: It does not matter. We have arranged a date for you for tomorrow night

FABIOLA: With a handsome young internist: Dr. Diego.

PILAR: Dr. Diego?

ARMANDO: He is Doctor Mendoza's son.

PILAR: What if I already met someone?

ARMANDO: Who have you met? Where?

PILAR: At the park. I do not know his name.

ARMANDO: If I do not know him or his family–he might as well not exist. Doctor Diego will make a good and prosperous husband.

PILAR: I do not want a husband! I do not want a rose dress! I do not want blonde hair! I want to go to school!

ARMANDO: What am I doing wrong with this child?

FABIOLA: You spoil her, Armando.

ARMANDO: She is still young.

FABIOLA: There you go again, making excuses for her. Just like you did with your lazy good for nothing son Sebastián.

ARMANDO: Stop hurling that accusation at me. I threw out my son fifteen years ago at your urging.

PILAR: Please stop fighting.

FABIOLA: Life is a fight, Pilar! When my rich father died in that horrible fire, I had to make my own way in this cruel world.

Now is the time to use the fading gifts I gave you. By the time I was your age, I was already married to the most powerful man in Bellarica and pregnant with you.

PILAR: And that is your desire for your daughter? To be as unhappy and trapped as you?

ARMANDO: *(Temper flares.)* ENOUGH, Pilar!

FABIOLA: My God!

PILAR: Sorry, Papi.

ARMANDO: You are my daughter. You carry my name. My duty is to protect you. And you–you have a responsibility to me, to your mother, and to God…to honor us. To obey us!

FABIOLA: Do you understand?

PILAR: Yes. I understand.

THE SADDEST SONG: A ROSE IN THE DESERT

PILAR *(CONT'D)*: Sand rolls in like an ocean
Waves of heat and despair
A seed lies buried in darkness
And no one knows she's there

VICTORIA: Cold and cruel is the night-time
Cold and cruel is the nighttime
Fierce and hot is the day
A drop of rain is all she needs
To dream of a better way

BOTH: Heart of hope in a petal
Thorns that cut like a knife
Tonight she will not break
She will fight for her life

A rose that blooms in the desert
Is a flower fighting for her life
She is a rose in the desert…

The mansion scene freezes or goes into very slow motion. A jail cell is pushed out by COP 2 (DR. DIEGO).

HORTENCIA sits in jail in handcuffs. VICTORIA is visiting.

VICTORIA: Mami–I am here to confess my crime.

HORTENCIA: Quiet! Never say that again. Your father and I have worked too hard, and love you too much to watch you wither away and die in a prison cell. Do you hear me?

VICTORIA: I hear you. I see you.

She clenches her heart.

HORTENCIA: Breathe. Breathe. Catch your breath. You must remember to take your medicines. If you die, I die. You have to stay healthy for me, for your father. For our family.

VICTORIA: This is destroying our family. Papi is devastated by your affair with Dr. Mendoza…

HORTENCIA: *(Beat.)* Forgive me.

VICTORIA: Doctor Mendoza is very handsome.

HORTENCIA: And your father…was so busy…and the doctor was very persistent. And I am weak.

VICTORIA: *(Beat.)* You never had an affair. Did you?

HORTENCIA: I was tempted, perhaps, but I never yielded.

VICTORIA: What are we going to do, Mami?

HORTENCIA: The judge might be lenient for a poor woman like me.

VICTORIA: What if Dr. Mendoza dies? The judge could decide to make a terrible example out of you and lock you up forever.

HORTENCIA: Nothing in life is certain…except your father's and my love for you.

VICTORIA: I am going to go to the Castillo house.

HORTENCIA: You should tell them I am in jail. And please tell my sweet poet Pilar not to worry.

VICTORIA: I am going to ask Fabiola Castillo for your job.

HORTENCIA: No! You will not be a maid. Your destiny is not to scrub her sad floors and wash her bitter dishes. You are to go to the University.

VICTORIA: Mami–we need money for a lawyer to get you out of jail.

HORTENCIA: You have dreamed of being a doctor since you were little. You need to have the full life your father and I have worked so hard to give you.

VICTORIA: I will live my life fully as a maid. Just like you.

HORTENCIA: Why do you defy me?

VICTORIA: Because you are my mother!!

Beat.

And because I love you.

HORTENCIA bursts into tears.

HORTENCIA: Oh, Victoria. No!

*ACTOR *(COP 2/DIEGO)*: The United States imprisons more people than any other nation in the world. About one out of everyone hundred Americans is behind bars.

The prison retreats. VICTORIA is at the front door. The door bell rings.

FABIOLA: Hortencia!!! Open the door.

The bell rings again.

FABIOLA AND ARMANDO: Hortencia!!!

FABIOLA: Where is she?

PILAR: She has that sick daughter…

Doorbell again.

ARMANDO: We should fire her. Hire someone younger.

FABIOLA: You would like that, I am sure.

Doorbell again…

There is no one to open the door!

PILAR: I will open it.

PILAR opens the door. Sees VICTORIA. There is a connection. A chord of music.

VICTORIA: I am Victoria Maria, Hortencia's daughter.

PILAR: Victoria! Come in.

Hugs her.

I am Pilar Esperanza. Hortencia has told me so much about you.

VICTORIA: Pilar! I have heard so many stories about you. I feel like you are…my long-lost sister.

PILAR: Me too! I am so glad we finally meet. Is everything all right?

FABIOLA: Who is it, Pilar?

She sees VICTORIA.

Oh! My God.

(Beat.)

It is you!

VICTORIA: Hello Señora Castillo. Perhaps you know me? I am Hortencia's daughter.

FABIOLA: Hortencia's daughter. So you are.

(Music. A stare. Lights out. Rewind. Lights back on. Music. Repeat to same place.)

FABIOLA *(CONT'D)*: Who is it, Pilar?–Oh! My God.

Beat.

It is You!

VICTORIA: Hello Señora Castillo. Perhaps you know me?

Beat.

I am Hortencia's daughter.

FABIOLA: Hortencia's daughter. So you are.

(Holds her face in her hands.)

Such grace…and such frailty. If only I had known.

You are nothing and everything I imagined.

VICTORIA: Excuse me?

ARMANDO: Who do we have here, Fabiola?

FABIOLA: This is…Hortencia's daughter.

PILAR: Victoria Maria…

ARMANDO: I have seen you before.

FABIOLA: Armando, you would never know someone like her.

136

ARMANDO: But I have seen those eyes before. I never forget beauty.

VICTORIA: Perhaps they look like my mother's?

ARMANDO: That must be it.

VICTORIA: My mother is…not well. So, I have come in her place for the time being…

FABIOLA: I am afraid this arrangement will not work.

VICTORIA: Please Señora, I will do a good job.

FABIOLA: Leave!

PILAR: Stay! Papi, Mami, Victoria could help me at the Ball… She could be my assistant.

VICTORIA: I work hard. My mother has taught me well.

FABIOLA: Child, do not pretend. I know you have a weak heart.

VICTORIA: *(Grabs FABIOLA'S hands.)* Please Señora. I assure you, my heart is strong. It has never stopped me from working. I just have to be careful.

PILAR: Why deny Victoria the chance to help us and us the chance help her?

FABIOLA: Because…because…your father…

ARMANDO: I have decided. Victoria will stay. She must wear a maid's uniform as soon as possible.

PILAR: Thank you, Papi.

FABIOLA: Armando–

ARMANDO: *(Cuts her off.)* That means, Pilar, you must go to the Charity Ball and please your mother.

PILAR: Mami, I will go to the Ball tomorrow night.

FABIOLA: And you will be charming to your date Dr. Diego. At midnight, you will be crowned Princess of the Ball.

PILAR: In front of everybody?

FABIOLA: Victoria, if Pilar fails in any way, you will be fired immediately.

VICTORIA: Señora. I promise I will exceed your expectations.

FABIOLA: I fear you already have, my child. Excuse me.

FABIOLA exits.

ARMANDO: My daughter must represent the elegance and class of the Castillo family. Now change out of that dress. It cheapens you.

PILAR: Yes, Papi.

VICTORIA: Thank you Pilar. Thank you, Señor Castillo.

ARMANDO: You will call her Señorita Pilar.

VICTORIA: Yes, sorry Señorita Pilar.

PILAR exits.

ARMANDO: Do not be familiar. You should know your place. After all, you are only a maid.

And he taps VICTORIA's bottom.

And I am your boss.

*ACTOR *(PILAR)*: In the United States, 65 % of minimum wage workers are women and more than half of them experience sexual harassment at work.

SCENE 5: SECRETS AND LIES

The hospital. DOCTOR MENDOZA is wheeled in his gurney by PARAMEDIC 1 (SEBASTIÁN).

*ACTOR *(ARMANDO): (With placard:)* Secrets and lies.

> *DOCTOR MENDOZA tries to rise from his gurney, SISTER SONIA shoves him back down. They glare at one another. Suddenly DOCTOR DIEGO enters in a rush. DOCTOR MENDOZA lies down quickly to keep the scene going.*

DOCTOR DIEGO: I just heard my father was shot. What happened?

SISTER SONIA: Doctor Diego, your father…was shot.

> *Music.*

DOCTOR DIEGO: How could such a terrible thing happen?

SISTER SONIA: He was attacked while visiting a poor family with a sick daughter.

DOCTOR DIEGO: Why would anyone shoot their doctor?

SISTER SONIA: The world is a complicated place.

DOCTOR DIEGO: My father and I are estranged. But I will take good care of him now.

SISTER SONIA: Your father is in a deep coma. He is hovering between life and death. I should call the Priest.

DOCTOR DIEGO: My father is a robust and healthy man. If anyone can survive this, he can.

*ACTOR *(PARAMEDIC 1)*: Latinos in the United States have a higher life expectancy than white or black Americans despite lower wages and poor access to healthcare. This is called the Hispanic Paradox.

139

SISTER SONIA: Let us hope he will awake one day. Nothing is impossible.

DOCTOR DIEGO: Sister, you know him better than I do. Is my father a good man?

SISTER SONIA: *(Beat.)* He is a skilled Doctor.

DOCTOR DIEGO: He was always working. My mother and I rarely saw him. But is he a good man?

SISTER SONIA: Dr. Mendoza takes great pleasure in the prestige of being a doctor.

DOCTOR DIEGO: He is disappointed in me. When I went into medicine, he expected I would help him bolster his practice and elite clientele.

SISTER SONIA: Your work with the poor has made a great difference in the community, Dr. Diego.

DOCTOR DIEGO: I have an impossible dream of building a clinic that provides free medical help to the people who most need it.

SISTER SONIA: You are very different men.

DOCTOR DIEGO: But my father was helping that poor family with their daughter. Surely, that speaks to his goodness.

SISTER SONIA: I should call the Priest. We need to pray for his soul.

SISTER SONIA exits.

DOCTOR DIEGO: Father, I promise that despite our differences, I will do everything in my power to save your life.

FABIOLA enters.

FABIOLA: Doctor Diego?

DOCTOR DIEGO: Apologies, Señora, this room is private. May I help you?

FABIOLA: I am Fabiola Castillo.

DOCTOR DIEGO: Oh!

Beat.

Of course, you have raised so much money for this hospital.

FABIOLA: I am here to remind you that you are escorting my daughter, Pilar Esperanza, to the Castillo Charity Ball tomorrow night, Doctor.

DOCTOR DIEGO: I have other responsibilities, Señora Castillo. I am a doctor.

FABIOLA: You and Pilar will make an elegant couple at the Ball. Dr. Mendoza gave me his word you would come.

DOCTOR DIEGO: Señora. How will I recognize your daughter?

FABIOLA: She will be the only girl dressed in rose. Dear God, is that Dr. Mendoza?

DOCTOR DIEGO: Yes. My father is in a coma.

FABIOLA: What happened?

DOCTOR DIEGO: He was shot at a poor farm on the outskirts of town.

FABIOLA: Crime is such a blight in that area.

DOCTOR DIEGO: He is stable now but there is no indication he will regain consciousness.

SISTER SONIA: *(Offstage, as an intercom:)* Dr. Mendoza, Dr. Diego Mendoza, to the ER.

DOCTOR DIEGO: Excuse me, Señora Castillo. I must go.

FABIOLA: So, I will see you at the casino tomorrow night?

DOCTOR DIEGO: For once, I will honor my father's wish.

He exits.

FABIOLA: Dr. Mendoza. What a shame. But sometimes fate punishes you for your greed. I promised you some equipment, and then, you wanted more: a new department, a new wing! What next? A new building? I am tired of raising money for you and your hospital. I chose to help a poor child and you blackmail me for my kindness.

Whispers in his ear.

I hope you never wake up, Doctor!

FABIOLA hears someone stir/come in.

Who is there?

ERNESTO enters.

ERNESTO: Hello Fabiola.

Music.

FABIOLA: Ernesto! Did you shoot him?

ERNESTO: No. My daughter was holding the gun and it went off accidently.

FABIOLA: Victoria shot Dr. Mendoza?

ERNESTO: My wife Hortencia took the blame and has been arrested. But if Dr. Mendoza dies…

FABIOLA: …your wife will rot in jail forever

ERNESTO: And there will be no one to care for my daughter's heart.

FABIOLA: How terrible!

ERNESTO: Since when do you care about me and my family?

FABIOLA: Your wife is my maid.

ERNESTO: Fabiola, You are the only secret I keep from my wife.

FABIOLA: Good! We should both forget our past.

ERNESTO: Help me get Hortencia out of jail. Or I will tell Armando you are not the daughter of a wealthy ranch owner.

FABIOLA: We lived on a ranch.

ERNESTO: As poor farm hands. And then you set that terrible fire... that burnt everything!

FABIOLA: You know what that ranch owner did to me! How I suffered! He deserved to die!

ERNESTO: That is why I took the blame and went to prison in your place.

FABIOLA: Your kindness has always been your greatest strength, Ernesto.

ERNESTO: I will tell the truth to save Hortencia.

FABIOLA: You can say what you want. Armando will never believe you.

ERNESTO: I am still a poor farmer. You are now rich and blonde. But you can't hide from the truth!

SISTER SONIA: *(Offstage as intercom:)* Ernesto. Ernesto del Rio. To the billing and cashier's department

FABIOLA: Get out!

ERNESTO: You must do everything in your power to make sure this son-of-a-bitch doctor does not die.

ERNESTO exits.

FABIOLA: I hate you.

SISTER SONIA enters.

Sister Sonia! I was just leaving. I was only here to–

SISTER SONIA: To visit your accomplice?

FABIOLA: To invite Doctor Diego to the Castillo Ball.

SISTER SONIA: Dr. Mendoza is in a coma. Hortencia del Rio is in jail. What you did eighteen years ago has had terrible consequences.

FABIOLA: You cannot blame me for everything!

SISTER SONIA: Your daughter is alive because of Hortencia.

FABIOLA: Victoria is fine; she is working as a maid for me.

SISTER SONIA: If any harm comes to Victoria, I swear to God, I will tell Armando and the police your secret.

FABIOLA: Sister, are you threatening me?

SISTER SONIA: Yes I am.

(As she is about to exit:) I heard your step–son was at church earlier today.

FABIOLA: That cannot be! Armando banished Sebastián from Bellarica fifteen years ago.

SISTER SONIA: Nothing is impossible, especially in Bellarica.

SISTER SONIA exits.

FABIOLA: Oh no. I must stop my world from unravelling.

SCENE 6: MORE SECRETS AND LIES

*ACTOR *(ARMANDO): (With placard:)* More secrets and lies.

A hotel room. SEBASTIÁN is getting dressed. FABIOLA opens the door to his hotel room and rushes in.

FABIOLA: Oh, Sebastián!

SEBASTIÁN: Fabiola!

FABIOLA: You cannot be here in Bellarica.

SEBASTIÁN: Fabiola…you should not be in my room.

FABIOLA: This is too dangerous.

Beat.

I have missed you so much!

She takes off her jacket.

SEBASTIÁN: Our last meeting in Monterrey was three months ago.

She pounces on him on the bed and mounts him. He wants to resist… but… the resolve is difficult.

FABIOLA: But if Armando finds you here, he will destroy us.

SEBASTIÁN: I know. Fabiola…I cannot go on like this any longer.

FABIOLA pulls off his belt.

Beat.

FABIOLA: What are you saying?

SEBASTIÁN: Fabiola, we need to end this.

FABIOLA: You said I was beautiful.

SEBASTIÁN: You are as beautiful as ever.

FABIOLA: Touch me. Feel me. My skin, my lips, my body are all yours.

She ties him with her belt.

SEBASTIÁN: I cannot deny the desire I feel for you but I want something more.

FABIOLA: One day Armando will die and everything will be ours.

SEBASTIÁN: I do not want my father to die. Not anymore.

FABIOLA: Go to Monterrey! Wait for me at our favorite hotel.

SEBASTIÁN: I want to come home, Fabiola. Today…I caught a glimpse of what my life could be… If I made a change.

FABIOLA: Me too. I love you.

Stops her.

SEBASTIÁN: This is not how love feels.

FABIOLA: Another woman? Who is it? I will kill her.

SEBASTIÁN: I do not know her name. But with her, I realized that I want to be a better man. And the first step is to end this and make peace with my father.

FABIOLA: After Armando disowned you and threw you out on the street?

SEBASTIÁN: I will ask his forgiveness. I have a plan involving online technology that will generate new revenue streams for the Castillo Casino. My father may be proud but he still wants to be rich.

FABIOLA: Oh Sebastián, for years you asked me to run away with you. I was stupid to say no.

SEBASTIÁN: Fabiola, you were right to refuse me. We were young and angry.

FABIOLA: I was seduced by an older man and suddenly married with a baby. And then I met his handsome son, only a year younger than me.

SEBASTIÁN: You were like fire, beautiful and dangerous. I burned for you.

FABIOLA: I fell deeply in love with you.

SEBASTIÁN: It is time to set ourselves free of the past.

FABIOLA: Oh Sebastián, one can never be free of the past.

FABIOLA sincerely cries for a moment.

SEBASTIÁN: I have never seen you cry.

FABIOLA: My heart aches for you.

Beat.

But, nothing this good can last forever.

SEBASTIÁN: And it will destroy us if we keep on. Think of my father. Think of your daughter.

FABIOLA: *(Bitterly.)* Pilar Esperanza.

SEBASTIÁN: My little sister. She was three years old the last time I saw her.

FABIOLA: Pilar is eighteen and a thorn in my side.

SEBASTIÁN: I would love to see her again.

FABIOLA: Promise you will never betray our secret to Armando.

*ACTOR *(ARMANDO)*: 68% of married women, in the United States say they would have an affair if they knew they would never get caught. [*Play location*] is in the United States.

FABIOLA: When he loves, he loves, but when he angers…God rest Sofia's soul.

SEBASTIÁN: My father did not kill my mother. He loved her dearly.

FABIOLA: I hope you are right.

SEBASTIÁN: I will never let any harm come your way, Fabiola.

FABIOLA: Thank you.

SEBASTIÁN: Forgive me.

FABIOLA: Goodbye.

She smiles sadly. She exits. The door closes behind her.

Music.

FABIOLA'S TANGO (PAIN MAKES ME BEAUTIFUL)
YOU LEFT ME
I WILL NEVER FORGET
YOU LEFT ME
I WILL NEVER FORGIVE
I'LL MAKE SURE YOU REPENT
YOU FOOLISH BOY
I'M NOT YOUR TOY
I'LL DRIVE YOU TO YOUR KNEES
I WILL IGNORE YOUR PLEAS
GO AHEAD SAY GOODBYE
WE WILL SEE WHO SURVIVES
BECAUSE
PAIN MAKES ME BEAUTIFUL

SCENE 7: SERVANTS, POETS…AND SISTERS?

*ACTOR *(DR. MENDOZA): (With placard:)* Servants, poets…and sisters?

The Mansion. PILAR's bedroom.

PILAR: Victoria. Come out. At once.

VICTORIA enters in a very short maid's uniform.

VICTORIA: It is time to get you ready for the Ball, Señorita Pilar.

PILAR: I do not want to go.

VICTORIA: We cannot let your mother down.

PILAR: Unfortunately, I do. All the time.

PILAR sits down and VICTORIA begins to brush her hair.

VICTORIA: Sit. My mother tells me you always relax when she brushes your hair.

PILAR: Oh Hortencia, I hope she feels better.

VICTORIA: My mother is not sick. She is in jail.

PILAR: No! What happened?

VICTORIA: She is accused of shooting Dr. Mendoza.

PILAR: Hortencia would never do such a thing.

VICTORIA: You are right.

VICTORIA starts to cry.

If only I could change the past.

PILAR: Let me help bear your sorrow.

VICTORIA: I came home to find a man threatening my father with a machete.

PILAR: A machete?

VICTORIA: So I grabbed a rifle.

PILAR: You shot Dr. Mendoza?

VICTORIA: Dr. Mendoza who has been nothing but good to me.

PILAR: You were just defending the people you love. The police will understand that.

VICTORIA: The world does not work like that. Not for people like me.

PILAR: Oh.

VICTORIA: My mother has taken the blame. Tonight, she is behind bars instead of me.

PILAR: Victoria, I envy you.

VICTORIA: What are you saying?

PILAR: No one loves me enough to sacrifice themselves like that for me.

VICTORIA: Surely, your father…your mother…

PILAR: My father dotes on me, but at his whim. And my mother is on a mission to smooth every angle and pummel every passion I have. I am nobody in my own house.

VICTORIA: I never imagined that you could be so lonely in this big beautiful house.

PILAR: Your mother cares. She gave me my first book of poetry.

VICTORIA: My mother says your poems are so vivid. Please, recite one for me.

PILAR: One day, I will love, and I will know no other way
Your tears will be my eyes, your laughter will be my mouth
Your heart will be my pulse.

VICTORIA: Your poems are beautiful, Señorita Pilar.

PILAR: Call me Pilar. You should not be anyone's servant, Victoria.

VICTORIA: I want to be a doctor and someday really help the poor in my neighborhood.

PILAR: I have a date with a doctor tonight.

VICTORIA: Oh, there's so much I would ask him.

PILAR: My parents want to marry me off as soon as they can.

VICTORIA: Let me get your new dress.

She pulls it out. It is as Cinderella-ish as it can be.

Rose.

PILAR: That dress is not me.

VICTORIA: The dress is lovely. I could never imagine wearing something like this.

PILAR: Why not?

VICTORIA: I am poor, Pilar.

PILAR: Oh.

VICTORIA: And I have scars.

PILAR: Scars? Where?

VICTORIA: I have had fifteen surgeries.

PILAR: For your heart? I do not see them.

VICTORIA: I am ashamed of them.

PILAR: Ashamed of your own skin? No. Never. Please, can I see them?

VICTORIA lifts her shirt and shows an angry red scar. PILAR reacts.

Does it hurt?

Pilar traces it.

VICTORIA: No.

PILAR: *(Spoken like a poet.)* A trail of where there was once pain.

VICTORIA: Pain that has passed. But the memory is ugly.

PILAR: *(Beat.)* I want you to try on this dress.

VICTORIA: No! I have never touched something so fine… before.

PILAR: Try it on, Victoria. Please. My mother is not here. It is just you and me.

VICTORIA disrobes and puts on the dress.

VICTORIA: Oh!

PILAR: This dress was destined for you.

VICTORIA: *(She dances.)* Is this me? Am I dancing?

She stops.

Oh… But you can see the scar on my chest. I need a scarf to cover the damage.

PILAR touches VICTORIA's scar.

PILAR: No. Your scars are your beauty. They are your jewelry.

Beat.

I have an idea.

VICTORIA: Wait, what are you doing?

PILAR quickly puts on VICTORIA's uniform.

PILAR: Tonight you will dance in my dress. And I will wear your uniform.

VICTORIA: But your parents! And your coronation?

PILAR: My parents will not look for me until midnight. We can change back before then.

VICTORIA: But. But.

PILAR: For eighteen years, Hortencia has told me stories about your family and I have dreamed of being you. Tonight you will be Pilar Esperanza.

VICTORIA: And you will be my maid, Victoria Maria.

PILAR: This promises to be an unforgettable night.

*ACTOR *(HORTENCIA)*: Peer pressure increases risky behavior among adolescents because their prefrontal cortex is still rapidly changing.

SCENE 8: TAKING A CHANCE ON LOVE

*ACTOR *(SISTER SONIA)* WITH PLACARD: Taking a chance on love.

The Casino. ARMANDO's Office.

SEBASTIÁN: Armando Castillo?

ARMANDO: *(Playing cards not looking up.)* Who dares call on me at my casino without an appointment or invitation? Especially on the night of my Charity Ball?

SEBASTIÁN: Your son.

ARMANDO: *(Turns.)* Sebastián?

SEBASTIÁN: You told me not to come back until I had made something of myself, Father.

ARMANDO: Have you changed, my son?

SEBASTIÁN: The reckless boy you threw out is gone.

ARMANDO: Do you hate me for what I did?

SEBASTIÁN: I did once but not anymore. Now I just want to be a better man.

ARMANDO: *(Dismissive.)* I must join Fabiola and greet all our guests as they enter the Ball.

SEBASTIÁN: I know the Casino is losing money.

ARMANDO: How dare you–

SEBASTIÁN: I have returned home to ask forgiveness from you and to bring prosperity to our family.

I have a plan involving online technology that will generate new revenue streams for the Castillo Casino.

He hands ARMANDO a business plan.

Your revenues will increase by 47%.

*ACTOR *(DR. MENDOZA)*: In the United States, Latinos control 1.3 trillion dollars in buying power accounting for half of the growth of home ownership and quarter of Toyota Corollas sold.

ARMANDO: A virtual casino…this looks very impressive.

SEBASTIÁN: It is more than impressive. It is effective.

ARMANDO: I will look it over. You should come by the house tomorrow. Say hello to your step-mother. Introduce yourself again to your sister.

SEBASTIÁN: I would like that. It has been a long time.

ARMANDO: I see your mother's warmth in your eyes. Sofia would be so proud of you right now.

SEBASTIÁN: Thank you. I miss Mother too.

ARMANDO: It is my great fortune to have you home, Sebastián.

SEBASTIÁN: I am happy to have my family again, father.

ARMANDO opens the door to the casino. A chandelier goes up. The Ball is exquisite.

ARMANDO: The Castillo Casino…in all its glory! Enjoy it, my son.

ARMANDO exits. PILAR and VICTORIA enter.

VICTORIA: This is the most elegant place I have ever seen! All the men in tuxedos and the women in beautiful gowns. Everyone is sparkling under the chandeliers.

PILAR: The Castillo Charity Ball is the highlight of the social season in Bellarica. The men come to parade their wives and the women come to display their jewels. Those are the high stakes tables, where fortunes are made and lost in the blink of an eye. All the money the house wins tonight goes to the hospital.

VICTORIA: This is a place for dreams.

(Suddenly realizing where she is.)

People will look at me and know I am a fraud.

PILAR: No one has looked at me at all.

VICTORIA: Because the poor are invisible.

PILAR: Oh. *(Seeing SEBASTIÁN.)* Oh–there is the man I told you about. Is he not handsome?

VICTORIA: He is dashing.

DOCTOR DIEGO walks in. He taps VICTORIA on the shoulder. A ripple of music.

DOCTOR DIEGO: I am Dr. Diego Mendoza. You must be the beautiful woman in rose I am supposed to dance with tonight.

VICTORIA: Oh me?

DIEGO: Pilar?

PILAR: Yes, it is she: Pilar.

DOCTOR DIEGO: Pilar, you seem surprised to see me.

VICTORIA: Yes, um–I

PILAR: We were not expecting the escorts so soon! It is fashionable to be late.

DOCTOR DIEGO: I think it is wise to be punctual when you have a date with Destiny. Do you like to gamble, Pilar?

VICTORIA: Would you believe me if I said I have never played in a casino before?

DOCTOR DIEGO: *(Laughs.)* I like you. The dancing has yet to start. Let us play Blackjack.

VICTORIA looks panicked at PILAR. DEALER pushes. Maybe the actors hold lights and make the sounds of slot machines or they are guests at the Casino. VICTORIA grabs PILAR to one side.

VICTORIA: What should I do, Pilar?

PILAR: Talk to him of course.

VICTORIA: I have never been on a date before.

PILAR: What?

DOCTOR DIEGO smiles at VICTORIA.

VICTORIA: Doctor Diego, do you know how to play Blackjack?

DOCTOR DIEGO: Of course. You have to hit twenty-one. Dealer…stay.

DEALER: Dealer wins.

DOCTOR DIEGO: Again. Hit me.

DEALER: Twenty-four – Dealer wins.

DOCTOR DIEGO: One last time.

DEALER: Dealer wins.

VICTORIA: Oh no.

DOCTOR DIEGO: They say, unlucky in cards, lucky in love. Your turn, Pilar.

VICTORIA: Me?

DOCTOR DIEGO: Of course!

PILAR pulls VICTORIA aside.

PILAR: Have you ever gambled before?

VICTORIA: I play Bingo with my father all the time.

PILAR: Oh my God!

DEALER: Señorita?

VICTORIA: Hit me.

DOCTOR DIEGO: I would wait if I were you.

PILAR: An eighteen is good, Señorita.

VICTORIA: Eighteen is not good enough. Hit me.

DEALER: Twenty–One. The young lady wins.

VICTORIA: Again. Hit me.

PILAR: A nineteen is very good, Señorita.

VICTORIA: Still not good enough. Hit me.

DEALER: Twenty One. The young lady wins.

DOCTOR DIEGO: Look at all the money you have won!

VICTORIA: One more round. All or nothing.

DEALER: If you lose, Señorita, you will have to pay in cash. And if you do not have cash, the casino has the right to confiscate your home, car, and furniture.

VICTORIA: Great. I have nothing to lose, do I?

DEALER: A Seven and a Jack.

VICTORIA: *(Stressful music.)* Dealer, hit me.

DOCTOR DIEGO: You should not tempt fate.

VICTORIA: Tonight, Doctor Diego, I refuse to play it safe.

*ACTOR *(SISTER SONIA)*: In the United States, women begin gambling later than men but develop problems and addiction more quickly.

VICTORIA: Dealer, hit me.

DEALER: Four!

Reaction.

VICTORIA: I won!

PILAR: You won!

VICTORIA: This money will help my Mami.

DEALER: Señorita, if you wish to continue, my boss Señor Castillo would like to meet you first.

DOCTOR DIEGO: Certainly, Armando Castillo would have no issue with his–

VICTORIA: Tell Señor Castillo, I am done playing for the night. I will cash out.

DOCTOR DIEGO: What an amazing streak of luck! Fortune is smiling on you tonight!

VICTORIA: I just did a quick calculation of the odds.

DOCTOR DIEGO: You were counting the cards!

VICTORIA: Of course! I mean otherwise the game is stacked against you.

DOCTOR DIEGO: Counting cards is a very rare skill. Did your father teach you?

VICTORIA: No. I just like math.

DOCTOR DIEGO: Me too! And I like science.

VICTORIA: I want to be a doctor.

DOCTOR DIEGO: I am a doctor.

VICTORIA: I feel like dancing, Doctor.

DOCTOR DIEGO: There is no music.

VICTORIA: There is. Can you not hear it?

MUSIC starts.

DOCTOR DIEGO and VICTORIA and SEBASTIÁN and PILAR romantically dance to THE MOST BEAUTIFUL SEXY SONG OF LOVE EVER. Wind blows. The casino lights twinkle like stars. Mesmerizing.

THE MOST BEAUTIFUL SEXY SONG OF LOVE EVER (SPANISH VERSION *CORAZÓN HERIDO…*)

VICTORIA *(CONT'D)*:

(Verse 1)
> VES LO QUE ME HACES?
> REVUELVES MI RAZÓN
> Y DEJAS QUE SE DESATEN
> MI DESEO Y MI TENTACIÓN

(Verse 2)
> ERES MI SUEÑO
> (YO) DE CARNE Y HUESO SOY
> PALPITA MI ALMA
> Y MI TODO TE LO DOY

(Pre-chorus 1)
> EL DON DE TU MIRADA
> HACE MI SANGRE LATIR
> EL PULSO DE TUS LABIOS
> RUEGA MI PIEL POR DECIR…

(Chorus)
> TÓCAME!
> BÉSAME!
> ÁMAME!
> LLÉNAME DE TU AMOR!
> PORQUE NEGAR TU CARIÑO
> ES UN CASTIGO SIN PERDÓN

TÓCAME!
BÉSAME!
ÁMAME!
LLENA MI CUERPO CON TU AMOR
DALE CALOR A MI VIDA
ANTES QUE MUERA DE PASIÓN
MI CORAZÓN HERIDO

PILAR is stunned by VICTORIA's glorious transformation. Dr. DIEGO is swinging her in the air.

PILAR: Oh my God.

SEBASTIÁN: Oh my God.

SEBASTIÁN taps PILAR's Shoulder. She turns and gasps.

PILAR: How are you here?

SEBASTIÁN: I am staying in the penthouse of the hotel. How are you here?

PILAR: I am a maid in Armando Castillo's house. Are you disappointed?

SEBASTIÁN: You are a poet who works as a maid?! Shall we dance as well?

PILAR: Yes!

DOCTOR DIEGO: CUMBIA!

(Verse 3)
QUITAME EL MIEDO
ENVUELVEME EN TU AMOR
QUIERO EN TU FUEGO
QUEMARME SIN TEMOR

VICTORIA:

(Verse 4)

> MIRA LAS CICATRICES
> DE MI POBRE CORAZÓN
> SÁNAME LAS HERIDAS QUE
> ATORMENTAN MI RAZÓN

VICTORIA & PILAR:

(Pre–chorus 1)

> SIENTE EL CALOR DE MI ALMA
> Y MI PROFUNDA PASIÓN
> TUS BESOS SON MI AIRE
> RESPIRAME ENTERA, CORAZÓN

ALL:

(Chorus)

> TÓCAME!
> BÉSAME!
> ÁMAME!
> LLÉNAME DE TU AMOR!
> PORQUE NEGAR TU CARIÑO (?)
> ES UN CASTIGO SIN PERDÓN
> TÓCAME!
> BÉSAME!
> ÁMAME!
> LLENA MI CUERPO CON TU AMOR
> DALE CALOR A MI VIDA
> ANTES QUE MUERA DE PASIÓN

VICTORIA: MI CORAZÓN HERIDO

End of song. Some slow dancing.

SEBASTIÁN: Do you remember the promise you made about the next time we met?

PILAR: Yes, I do.

SEBASTIÁN: May I?

PILAR kisses him. They are amazed by the connection. The clock starts to ring twelve.

PILAR: Oh no! It is midnight.

Pilar starts to run. SEBASTIÁN grabs her hand.

SEBASTIÁN: What is your name?

PILAR: *(Tries to get VICTORIA's attention.)* Victoria Maria! Midnight!

PILAR runs off.

SEBASTIÁN. Victoria Maria Midnight! Wait!

He runs after her. The last chimes of the clock.

VICTORIA: Midnight!

DR. DIEGO: The magical hour of your coronation.

VICTORIA and Dr. DIEGO are about to kiss. FABIOLA opens the door.

FABIOLA: Pilar!

VICTORIA: Señora Castillo!

VICTORIA runs off and leaves behind a shoe. DIEGO starts to run off after her.

FABIOLA: Dr. Diego! My daughter's shoe.

DIEGO takes the shoe and goes after VICTORIA.

DIEGO: Wait Pilar. Pilar!

DIEGO exits.

FABIOLA: My daughter.

REWIND! The whole scene repeats. The last bells chime.

VICTORIA: Midnight!

DR. DIEGO: The magical hour of your coronation.

FABIOLA opens the door.

FABIOLA: Pilar!

VICTORIA: Señora Castillo!

VICTORIA runs off and leaves behind a shoe. DIEGO starts to run off after her.

FABIOLA: Dr. Diego! My daughter's shoe.

DIEGO takes the shoe and exits after VICTORIA.

DIEGO: Wait Pilar. Pilar!

FABIOLA: My daughter.

SISTER SONIA walks in.

SISTER SONIA: God works in mysterious ways.

FABIOLA: Sister Sonia, what is a nun doing here at the Casino?

SISTER SONIA: I am here to tell Armando Castillo the truth.

ARMANDO opens the door holding a crown.

ARMANDO: Tell Armando what truth?

FABIOLA: Armando!

ARMANDO: Sister Sonia!

SISTER SONIA: Señor Castillo!

ARMANDO: It is midnight! Where is my daughter?

Looks.

And where is her maid?

FABIOLA: Gone! We have to find them.

FABIOLA drags ARMANDO off. Thunder. A storm is coming.

SISTER SONIA: I think a storm is coming.

SCENE 9: A SURPRISING TURN OF EVENTS

*ACTOR *(SEBASTIÁN): (With placard:)* A surprising turn of events.

At the Mansion. PILAR paces nervously, waiting for VICTORIA, who rushes in happily.

PILAR: Victoria! Where were you? I was worried. A terrible storm has started.

VICTORIA hugs PILAR.

VICTORIA: Your mother saw me!

PILAR: Oh no!

VICTORIA: She was so kind. She gave Dr. Diego my shoe.

PILAR: She did?

VICTORIA: And then Dr. Diego drove me home!

PILAR: Dr. Diego!

VICTORIA: Doctor Diego is beautiful. He believes me to be Pilar Esperanza Castillo.

PILAR: The doctor is very smitten with you. I saw you dancing with him.

VICTORIA: Oh God. My blood is rushing through my body. Did you see the money I won to help my mother?

PILAR: You are on fire!

VICTORIA: So are you. I saw you kissing that man you pointed out to me.

PILAR: Oh God! Yes. Yes yes! He believes I am a poet who works as a maid. He kissed me. I prayed for him to never stop. I wanted more.

VICTORIA: What is his name?

PILAR: I don't know! He is staying at the penthouse in the Casino.

VICTORIA: I kissed Doctor Diego. Again and again.

PILAR: No! "Pilar" kissed Doctor Diego again and again.

VICTORIA: Yes! And Pilar feels so free. And frantic. And so happy.

PILAR: Me too.

VICTORIA: Thank you for letting me be you…for one night.

PILAR: So how do I kiss?

VICTORIA: Excuse me?

PILAR: Before tonight, had you ever been kissed before?

VICTORIA: Never.

PILAR: So how does PILAR kiss?

VICTORIA: Like this!

VICTORIA suddenly kisses PILAR. PILAR looks shocked.

Beat.

166

PILAR: Victoria…

VICTORIA: I am so sorry. It must be the wine I sipped. I am heady–I am

PILAR: I kiss more like this.

PILAR kisses VICTORIA. The girls laugh.

VICTORIA: Wow.

PILAR AND VICTORIA: That was a good kiss!

VICTORIA: Thank you. I know so little. The only real romantic kissing I have ever seen is on telenovelas.

PILAR: They always do it like this. Resolute and passionate.

PILAR practices a Passionate Soap Opera Kiss on VICTORIA. They stop. Look out.

*ACTOR *(HORTENCIA)*. In the United States, 56% of girls have kissed another girl.

PILAR and VICTORIA kiss again.

And liked it.

VICTORIA: That was great. Let me try.

PILAR: Very passionate. Would Doctor Diego like this?

Kisses her.

VICTORIA: I am sure he would. How would your mystery man like this?

More practice kisses. ARMANDO bursts in. Lightning.

ARMANDO: What in the devil's name is going on here?

PILAR: Forgive me, Papi. We were just playing…

VICTORIA: Señor Castillo!

Suddenly ARMANDO smacks VICTORIA.

ARMANDO: What have you done to my daughter? What have you done?

He raises his hand to smack VICTORIA again.

PILAR: Papi, do not hurt her.

ARMANDO: You missed your own coronation!

ARMANDO turns and smacks PILAR to the ground. He turns back to VICTORIA.

VICTORIA: Señor, please do not hit her.

ARMANDO: You filth. Not in my house. Not between maidens. And maids. I will kill you.

VICTORIA back away from a furious ARMANDO. FABIOLA enters. More lightning.

He lunges at VICTORIA again. FABIOLA stops him by wrapping her arms around VICTORIA.

FABIOLA: Armando, do not hurt her!

ARMANDO: Fabiola–what are you doing?

FABIOLA realizes she is holding Victoria. She lets go of her and backs away.

FABIOLA: She is just a young girl.

VICTORIA's heart starts to fail.

PILAR: Breathe, Victoria. Breathe.

ARMANDO: She insulted me in my own house. Get her out of here.

Storm gets more intense. VICTORIA starts to have trouble with her heart.

PILAR: But the storm is dangerous. Mami, she will die out there. Help her.

ARMANDO: Victoria, get out of my sight now!

FABIOLA: Armando, the sand is blinding out there.

ARMANDO: Why are you defending her?

FABIOLA is emotionally pulled in two directions.

PILAR: Mami, help her. Victoria is frail!

ARMANDO: Fabiola! Why are you defending her?

PILAR: Mami!

FABIOLA: Victoria Maria.

FABIOLA wraps her arms around VICTORIA and opens the door. The storm is raging outside. She hugs her.

ARMANDO: Fabiola!

FABIOLA: Good bye, my child.

FABIOLA throws her VICTORIA out… into the deadly storm.

VICTORIA: I am sorry.

VICTORIA exits, trying to breathe, a hand clenched on her chest like a prisoner to her execution. The door closes. PILAR rushes the door.

PILAR: Victoria!!!!

ARMANDO: I will lock you in your room until you calm down.

PILAR: Victoria will die in the desert!

FABIOLA: Her destiny is her destiny, Pilar.

The door closes.

PILAR: Victoria! Victoria Maria. My sister. What have I done?

ACTOR *(ERNESTO): (With placard:)* A break in the action.

END OF ACT 1

Act II

SCENE 1: SORROW AND LOSS

ACTOR *(ERNESTO)*: Previously, in Act I of 'Destiny of Desire'…

We go back to the last part of the last part of the last scene before the break…but from a different perspective.

ARMANDO: I will lock you in your room until you calm down.

PILAR: No! Mami, Victoria will die in the desert!

FABIOLA: Her destiny is her destiny, Pilar.

The door closes.

PILAR: Victoria! Victoria Maria. My sister. What have I done?

ACTOR *(FABIOLA): (With placard:)* Sorrow and loss.

A sandstorm. Actors make the noise and are taken over by sound design. A cloth can be used to make the storm. VICTORIA stumbles out in her torn rose dress…she walks in the desert in a storm. She is utterly alone. She is hurt in so many ways. She cries. She clutches her heart.

VICTORIA: I will not die in the desert. My mother needs me. I will dance in Dr. Diego's arms again! Oh Pilar Esperanza, what have we done? The sand blows and I cannot see.

PILAR braves the sandstorm…during the scene, she and VICTORIA get so close, and yet…are separated by the elements.

PILAR: *(Open the window. She sings operatically.)* VICTORIA!

VICTORIA

How the wind howls!

Operatically sings:

MARIA

VICTORIA

Oh Pilar, my sister. Please find me. I am lost in the storm. My heart cracks in my chest.

I cannot go on anymore.

Sings.

VICTORIA MARIA. VICTORIA MARIA.

PILAR walks off stage bracing against the elements.

VICTORIA: Pilar! That was your voice. I heard you! I am here. Please find me. Pilar!

(PILAR walks past VICTORA, blinded by the sand. PILAR exits.)

PILAR: VICTORIA MARIA.

VICTORIA: No. It was just the wind.

Her chest is in pain.

I am so far away from you. Far away from my parents. I am drowning in the sand. Devoured by the storm. No one can hear my cries! My fate is to die here, alone.

VICTORIA collapses on the ground. Everything stops. Victoria is dead. Silence.

*ACTOR *(FABIOLA)*: One person is found dead each day in the desert between the United States and Mexico.

Suddenly ERNESTO comes out swinging at the elements.

ERNESTO Victoria Maria! Victoria Maria!

(ERNESTO finds VICTORIA MARIA and he sings or speaks trying to save her. A song of urgency.)

VICTORIA'S LULLABY

ERNESTO:

OH, GOD
MY POOR DAUGHTER!
SHE LIES UPON THE SAND
SO STILL, SO QUIET
LET ME HOLD HER LITTLE HAND
OH, SHE SLEEPS, SHE DREAMS
OH, MY LITTLE GIRL
SHE'S AS COLD AS EARTH
MY BLOOD TURNS TO STONE
SHE'S FOREVER GONE
THIS IS OUR LAST LULLABY
I WILL NOT SAY GOODBYE
WAKE UP
OPEN YOUR EYES
WAKE UP
NO TIME FOR LULLABIES
WAKE UP
SOON THE SUN WILL RISE
AND THERE CAN BE NO TOMORROW
WITHOUT YOU
WAKE UP
MY CHILD
WAKE UP
/WAKE UP

ALL:

/VICTORIA...MARIA
VICTORIA ...MARIA

VICTORIA...MARIA
VICTORIA...MARIA

ERNESTO exits with VICTORIA MARIA in his arms.

SCENE 2: REGRETS OVER DRINKS

*ACTOR *(SISTER SONIA): (With placard:)* Regrets over drinks.

The Casino. ARMANDO is at the bar.

ARMANDO: Bartender...give me another. And make it a double.

DEALER/BARTENDER: Señor Castillo, you told me to never give you more than two. No matter what you said.

ARMANDO: Shut up or I will fire you.

DEALER/BARTENDER: A double coming up.

ARMANDO: I am still a man! I am still the boss!

ARMANDO slams down his shot glass. FABIOLA enters.

FABIOLA: Armando!

ARMANDO: Fabiola.

FABIOLA: You are drinking too much. You know what that does to your temper.

ARMANDO: This is my casino. My bar.

FABIOLA: The storm outside is relentless.

ARMANDO: Why did you defend that degenerate maid?

FABIOLA: What do you mean?

ARMANDO: Who is she to you?

FABIOLA: Armando, listen to yourself.

ARMANDO: What kind of animal am I? What kind of man hits women?

FABIOLA: Your daughter needs discipline.

ARMANDO: A man should not hit a woman even with the petal of a rose. What have I done?

FABIOLA: What did the girls do to anger you?

ARMANDO: They were laughing and dancing and kissing each other. That maid ruined everything.

FABIOLA: Your Pilar Esperanza…is not who you think she is. You spoil her.

ARMANDO: She is my daughter, Fabiola. I love her.

FABIOLA: She defies you. She insults your honor. She has brought shame on your house. For a maid. I think she has finally revealed her true self to you.

ARMANDO: Perhaps I can send her to a convent down South.

FABIOLA: A convent is full of women, Armando.

ARMANDO: What shall I do?

FABIOLA: Treat your children equally and throw her out. Write her out of your will. You should deal with her like you dealt with Sebastián.

ARMANDO: I was hasty in throwing out Sebastián. I lost my son for fifteen years.

FABIOLA: It was the right thing to do. He was a bad seed.

SEBASTIÁN walks in.

SEBASTIÁN: Father?

FABIOLA: Oh dear God!

ARMANDO: Sebastián!

FABIOLA: Sebastián! What a surprise!

ARMANDO: *(Embraces him.)* Sebastián, fifteen years have passed since you last saw one another, but I hope you remember your step-mother, Fabiola.

SEBASTIÁN: Hello, Fabiola.

FABIOLA: Sebastián. I barely recognize you. Fifteen years...

SEBASTIÁN: Fifteen years is a long time.

ARMANDO: Look, Fabiola, the prodigal son has returned.

SEBASTIÁN: I am making amends for the boy I once was.

ARMANDO: Fabiola, embrace your step-son.

FABIOLA hesitates, then melts into the hug, hungry to be in SEBASTIÁN's arms.

Are you alright, Fabiola?

FABIOLA: I feel a little weak. This is all so surprising.

ARMANDO: Sebastián, I looked over your business proposal. I think we should implement it.

SEBASTIÁN: That is wonderful, Father!

ARMANDO: And you will help me, my son. You will come back and live with us.

ARMANDO embraces him – FABIOLA starts to panic.

FABIOLA: So soon?

ARMANDO: Why not? I want him to help me grow our business.

FABIOLA: But we hardly know each other any more.

ARMANDO: Sebastián is family. Blood of my blood. It is time for us to open our hearts and let Sebastián in. Especially since Pilar is leaving.

SEBASTIÁN: Where is my little sister going?

FABIOLA: As far away as possible.

SEBASTIÁN: What?

FABIOLA: Pilar has misbehaved terribly. And we are teaching her a lesson.

SEBASTIÁN: What could she have possibly done?

ARMANDO: It is simply too horrible to describe.

FABIOLA: Pilar has deeply injured your father.

SEBASTIÁN: Did she lie to you, like I did? Did she steal your money, like I did? Did she bring public shame to the Castillo Casino, like I did?

ARMANDO: She did much worse.

SEBASTIÁN: Father, how will throwing her out and disowning her help her?

ARMANDO: You said yourself that it is the best thing that happened to you. You told me, that I helped make you into a man.

SEBASTIÁN: Thanks to you, I learned to survive but it is my mother that taught me about becoming a man.

FABIOLA: Sofia has been dead for twenty years.

SEBASTIÁN: I still remember my mother saying: A good man will always put the needs of others before his; I finally understand what she meant.

FABIOLA: *(Amazed and even more in love with SEBASTIÁN)* You truly have grown, Sebastián.

SEBASTIÁN: You must forgive Pilar. Do not send my sister away on a whim.

FABIOLA: How dare you! Armando, I refuse to have this insolent young man live with us! His sleeping under our roof will only bring us trouble.

ARMANDO: *(To FABIOLA)* He is my son! Blood of my blood. And so is my daughter Pilar.

To SEBASTIÁN.

Your sister has deeply offended me. But you are right, I can ill afford to lose her for fifteen years. I will tell her that if she repents, I am open to forgiving her.

ARMANDO exits.

FABIOLA: *(After him.)* Armando! You do not owe that ungrateful child anything.

Beat.

Looks at SEBASTIÁN.

My world is unraveling. You. And I. We must run away together late tonight.

SEBASTIÁN: What? No.

FABIOLA: I cannot live with you so close, and yet so far.

SEBASTIÁN: Fabiola, I want to stay here and to be part of the family again.

FABIOLA: If you stay, I will confess our secret to Armando.

SEBASTIÁN: Telling him about us would destroy everything.

FABIOLA: Armando will kill us both. Just like he did your mother.

SEBASTIÁN: My Father did not kill my mother.

FABIOLA: So he says. But we both know his temper. Be the real man you say you are or else...

SEBASTIÁN: You would not dare.

FABIOLA: Forget your father. Forget this casino. Forget your new love. Our entire destiny is in your hands, Sebastián.

She exits. SEBASTIÁN is devastated. He sings an old traditional Mexican song to himself, full of the pain of loss and longing, like 'Fallaste Corazón' by Cuco Sánchez. It is a deeply internal song. Classic ranchera, all in Spanish. He should be weeping by the end.

*ACTOR (ERNESTO): Mexico is the largest Spanish-speaking country in the world. The United States is the second.

SCENE 3: ANOTHER SURPRISING TURN OF EVENTS

*ACTOR (HORTENCIA): (With placard:) Another surprising turn of events. Deal with it!

The hospital. Sounds of a hospital. DOCTOR MENDOZA connected to machines. DOCTOR DIEGO tends to him.

DOCTOR DIEGO: Father? Can you hear me? I met the most amazing woman. Her name is Pilar. She is the daughter of Fabiola and Armando Castillo.

DOCTOR MENDOZA starts to move. The beeping starts to accelerate. SISTER SONIA enters.

My father is squeezing my hand!

SISTER SONIA: We should thank God for this miracle!

DOCTOR DIEGO: Oh God, allow me to have a second chance to speak with my father. Father?

SISTER SONIA: *(Checking DOCTOR MENDOZA's eyes.)* Alas, no response. His coma remains deep.

ERNESTO runs in with VICTORIA in his arms.

ERNESTO: Help me, Doctor!

SISTER SONIA: Oh my God!

ERNESTO: She was lost in a sandstorm in the desert. But I found her.

DOCTOR DIEGO: *(He takes VICTORIA's pulse.)* I can detect a faint pulse… My God! It is Pilar. The woman with whom I danced at the Casino.

SISTER SONIA: Pilar?

DOCTOR DIEGO: Pilar Esperanza! She is the daughter of Armando Castillo.

SISTER SONIA: Doctor, you speak a truth and a lie at the same time.

ERNESTO: This is my daughter. Victoria Maria del Rio. She works as a maid at the Castillo household.

DOCTOR DIEGO: That cannot be true!

SISTER SONIA: She is the sick young lady your father was treating.

DOCTOR DIEGO: Was my father shot at your house?

ERNESTO: It was an accident. The person who shot him… intended no harm!

DOCTOR DIEGO: Dear God! My father may never wake again!

ERNESTO: Please, my daughter needs your help.

SISTER SONIA: Should I call another doctor, Doctor?

Beat.

DOCTOR DIEGO: I will help her. Sister Sonia, hand me Victoria Maria's charts.

(DOCTOR DIEGO listens to VICTORIA's heart.)

ERNESTO: Thank you, Doctor

DOCTOR DIEGO: Her heart is failing!

SISTER SONIA hands DOCTOR DIEGO the charts.

ERNESTO: What can we do?

DOCTOR DIEGO: *(Looking at charts.)* According to these charts, your daughter has been in urgent need of a heart transplant for years. But many of her surgeries seem to be medically unnecessary.

SISTER SONIA: Oh God have mercy!

ERNESTO: My wife kept asking Dr. Mendoza to look into a heart transplant.

DOCTOR DIEGO: And?

ERNESTO: Dr. Mendoza always dismissed her.

DOCTOR DIEGO: She is scarred all over from surgeries that she did not need. But the operation she needed most, she never received.

ERNESTO: I am a poor and uneducated man; I believed everything Dr Mendoza said. Oh my God, I did not protect you enough. Forgive me, my daughter. I have failed you as a father.

SISTER SONIA: Señor del Río, you took Victoria to school everyday. You worked long nights to support her. You listened to her dreams of the future. You taught her to believe in her intelligence and her kindness.

ERNESTO: But it is of no use. My child is dying. And once she does, Hortencia will die of grief in prison. And I...I...will lose all reason to live.

DOCTOR DIEGO: I can think of no better father. Señor del Río, we will stabilize her until we can find her a new heart. I will not let her die.

*ACTOR *(VICTORIA)*: On average, twenty-two people die each day waiting for a transplant. One donor could save eight lives.

ERNESTO: I will come with you, Doctor...

DOCTOR DIEGO exits with VICTORIA, ERNESTO.

SISTER SONIA: Oh poor child, what you have suffered! May God keep you in his mercy.

DOCTOR MENDOZA suddenly sits up.

DOCTOR MENDOZA: Nurse. Nurse.

SISTER SONIA: Dr. Mendoza! You are awake!

DOCTOR MENDOZA: Where am I?

SISTER SONIA: In the hospital.

DOCTOR MENDOZA moans.

Your son, Dr. Diego has been attending to you. We never expected you to wake so soon.

DOCTOR MENDOZA: The last thing I knew I was asking Hortencia del Río to marry me.

SISTER SONIA: Ah. And what did she say?

DOCTOR MENDOZA: She said no.

SISTER SONIA: Hortencia is in jail.

DOCTOR MENDOZA: For what?

SISTER SONIA: For shooting you.

DOCTOR MENDOZA: What! She did not shoot me. Hortencia is innocent. I need to get her out of jail.

SISTER SONIA: That is the right thing to do, Doctor.

DOCTOR MENDOZA: I will tell them it was Victoria Maria who shot me.

SISTER SONIA: Doctor Mendoza, if you had died, you would have gone straight to hell for all you have done to that girl.

DOCTOR MENDOZA: But she shot me! I am the victim.

SISTER SONIA: The only way to save your soul is to absolve Victoria Maria of any blame. If you do not, I will tell Armando how you and Fabiola switched his child at birth.

DOCTOR MENDOZA: How dare you!

SISTER SONIA: I will make sure you lose everything.

DOCTOR MENDOZA: Write down my statement.

SISTER SONIA takes out a pen and paper.

I, Doctor Jorge Ramiro Mendoza, son of Doctor Roberto Mendoza Escalante, grandson of Doctor Gonzalo Mendoza Monteverde y Luna, swear that Hortencia del Rio did not shoot me.

SISTER SONIA: That is not enough.

DOCTOR MENDOZA: It was an unfortunate accident …that I brought on myself.

SISTER SONIA: Now sign it. I am going to take this statement to the police.

DOCTOR MENDOZA: What kind of nun are you?

SISTER SONIA: The best kind. You should know, your patient, Victoria, is dying.

DOCTOR MENDOZA: Victoria needs a new heart.

SISTER SONIA: You are her doctor…how could you not help the girl?

DOCTOR MENDOZA: And risk not seeing Hortencia every week?

SISTER SONIA: I will tell your son that you are out of your coma.

SISTER SONIA Leaves. There is a stirring. Maybe someone was listening.

DOCTOR MENDOZA: Who is there? Diego? Is that you?

ERNESTO comes in.

ERNESTO: Dr. Mendoza, I have prayed you would live. Sister Sonia told me you were awake. Thank you for exonerating my wife.

DOCTOR MENDOZA: I did what you could not. She will be released from jail tonight.

ERNESTO: Victoria Maria is dying.

DOCTOR MENDOZA: I know.

ERNESTO: Your son is trying to save her.

DOCTOR MENDOZA: He will fail. Victoria Maria was never supposed to live. Her life was always a gamble. You need to finally accept her fate.

ERNESTO: And just allow my daughter to die?

DOCTOR MENDOZA: When she dies, I will console Hortencia in her grief. Your wife will fall in love with me, the only man who ever truly helped her.

ERNESTO: And I just go back to my farm, alone?

DOCTOR MENDOZA: I do not care what happens to you! The world could swallow you up and nobody would notice. I only want Hortencia!

ERNESTO: That is what happens to people like me in a world such as yours.

DOCTOR MENDOZA: You poor people: all you do is suffer. That is your role. You never change. This is something my foolish and naïve son will never understand. He has wasted his time, his education, his career on people like you.

ERNESTO: Doctor, I am grateful to you for giving me the chance to protect the ones I love from selfish and evil people like you.

ERNESTO uses a pillow to suffocate THE DOCTOR. Heart monitor makes a long beep.

Once Hortencia is out of jail I will turn myself in.

ERNESTO rings an alarm and leaves. DOCTOR DIEGO runs in.

DOCTOR DIEGO: Father! Father! Stay with me. Stay!

SISTER SONIA runs in. DOCTOR DIEGO starts to weep.

SISTER SONIA: I find no pulse.

DOCTOR DIEGO: My father is dead.

SISTER SONIA: I am so sorry.

DOCTOR DIEGO: I do not know what I would have said to him. I do not think he was a good man.

SISTER SONIA looks at him, and says nothing.

Hand me his chart, Sister Sonia. Time of death...4 am.

Beat.

Wait. My father is O Negative.

SISTER SONIA: My God! He's a universal donor!

DOCTOR DIEGO: We have a transplant for Victoria Maria del Rio. Get the operating theatre ready for major surgery. Stat!

SISTER SONIA: I love divine justice.

SCENE 4: CLIMAX

*ACTOR *(DR. MENDOZA): (With placard:)* Climax.

The hotel room. SEBASTIÁN is packing his bags. PILAR is knocking madly on a door. SEBASTIÁN opens it.

PILAR: I had to find you.

SEBASTIÁN: It is the middle of the night.

PILAR: I am sorry but I need your help to find my friend.

SEBASTIÁN: You are covered in sand. Your hair. Your lashes.

He gently wipes the sand away.

PILAR: You must help me!

SEBASTIÁN: What can I do?

PILAR: *(Grabs his hand.)* Come with me.

SEBASTIÁN: You are trembling.

PILAR: I am so cold.

He wraps his arms around her.

SEBASTIÁN: Let me warm you up.

He picks her up and lies her on the bed.

You have cuts and scratches all over.

He kisses them.

PILAR: My new jewelry.

They kiss.

SEBASTIÁN: Victoria.

PILAR: Please do not say that name!

SEBASTIÁN: Why? I love your name. Victoria. Maria!

PILAR: Please, just let me feel your heart against mine!

A beautiful choreographed love-making scene – with his bare chest, and wind and flowing satin sheets. And falling rose petals. Lots of rose petals. 'THE MOST BEAUTIFUL BALLAD IN THE WORLD EVER, MY WOUNDED HEART' is sung. Again–but differently: Hotter. Sadder. And in English.

THE MOST BEAUTIFUL SEXY SONG OF LOVE EVER

English Reprise of *Mi Corazón Herido–My Wounded Heart*

PILAR *(CONT'D)*: TAKE ALL OF MY SADNESS
STRIP AWAY MY FEAR
LIFE IS A MADNESS
IN YOU, I DISAPPEAR

SEBASTIÁN: THE PULSE OF YOUR HEARTBEAT
THE WILD LOOK IN YOUR EYES
THE WARMTH OF YOUR BODY

TEMPTATION WILL ARISE

PILAR: COME TO ME
BE WITH ME
STAY WITH ME
LET YOUR LOVE FILL ME DEEP INSIDE

SEBASTIÁN: TOUCH ME
AND KISS ME
AND LOVE ME
DEEP IN YOUR HEART I WANT TO HIDE

Requisite instrumental love-making break. Rain of roses.

BOTH: TAKE ME
AND LOSE ME
AND FIND ME
I'M ON MY KNEES, I HAVE NO PRIDE
HOLD ME
AND BURN ME
AND HEAL
MY WOUNDED HEART

SEBASTIÁN: Is everything all right?

PILAR: You are beautiful.

SEBASTIÁN: Did I hurt you?

PILAR: Today, I ruined someone's life. Someone who is good and kind.

SEBASTIÁN: Who?

PILAR: My best friend. I got caught up in a moment and–did things and said things. Now I cannot find her. If anything happens to her, it will be all my fault.

SEBASTIÁN: I will help you find your friend.

PILAR: Thank you!

PILAR kisses him. She sees his suitcases.

You were packing your bags. Are you leaving?

SEBASTIÁN: Yes. I have no choice. My business in Bellarica is finished.

PILAR: Oh.

SEBASTIÁN: I want you to come with me. I want to be with you.

PILAR: And I with you.

SEBASTIÁN: *(Kissing her.)* I think we should get married.

PILAR: We hardly know each other.

SEBASTIÁN: You have spent a night in my arms.

PILAR: You do not know me. I do not even know your name!

SEBASTIÁN kisses her when there is a LOUD KNOCK on the door. ARMANDO CASTILLO.

ARMANDO: My boy? Are you in there?

SEBASTIÁN AND PILAR: Armando Castillo!

PILAR: Oh my God! He cannot find me like this. I must hide.

SEBASTIÁN: Do not worry, Victoria, I will not let your boss fire you.

PILAR hides hopefully where we can still see her face.

ARMANDO: This is an emergency! Open up!

SEBASTIÁN opens the door.

SEBASTIÁN: What is the matter?

ARMANDO: I have to find Pilar Esperanza. I locked her in her room but she climbed out the third story window.

SEBASTIÁN: My God! Is she hurt?

ARMANDO: She disappeared into the storm! What kind of father drives his children away? You must help me find Pilar.

SEBASTIÁN: Father!

PILAR starts to silently freak out.

We shall find her. I will get dressed and meet you downstairs in the lobby, Father.

ARMANDO: Sebastián, please hurry. We must find your sister Pilar before it is too late!

ARMANDO walks out. PILAR starts to weep.

PILAR: Oh God!

SEBASTIÁN: I am sorry, Victoria, I promise I will help you find your friend when I return.

PILAR: Oh God! Oh God! You are Sebastián.

SEBASTIÁN: Yes. Sebastián Jose Castillo.

PILAR: Oh God!

SEBASTIÁN: Victoria, do not worry about your boss/

PILAR: /Oh God!

SEBASTIÁN: /Armando Castillo is my father/

PILAR: /Oh God!

SEBASTIÁN: /and he needs my help. My sister Pilar is in trouble…

PILAR: God help me! I am right here! Sebastián, I am your sister, Pilar.

SEBASTIÁN: No. You are Victoria Maria Midnight! You are a maid in my father's house.

PILAR: I am Pilar Esperanza Josefina. Daughter of Armando Castillo.

SEBASTIÁN: *(SEBASTIÁN is reeling with the news.)* Oh God.

PILAR: Victoria Maria is my maid. We were pretending to be each other at the Charity Ball.

SEBASTIÁN: Oh God!

PILAR: Victoria dressed like me…and I took her place as the maid.

SEBASTIÁN: Oh God! My half-sister.

PILAR. I am so sorry, Sebastián.

SEBASTIÁN: The prodigal son returns and ruins everything. I am a monster!

PILAR: The monster is me! First I destroy my friend. Then I destroy you.

SEBASTIÁN: I am a depraved man! I want to tear my heart out. And yet, as God is my witness, I have never loved a woman more than I love you.

PILAR: Sebastián! Stop! We can never be together!

SEBASTIÁN: Forgive me, Pilar. You offered me your innocence and I have destroyed us both.

PILAR: Oh Sebastián, forgive me.

They embrace. Door opens. Because doors never lock. It is FABIOLA with her suitcase.

FABIOLA: Sebastián. It is me!

SEBASTIÁN: Fabiola?

FABIOLA: Pilar?

PILAR: Mami?

FABIOLA: Sebastián!

SEBASTIÁN: Fabiola?

FABIOLA: What are the two of you doing here?

> *More heightened music. Lights out. Rewind. Moment of repeat like in Act 1. FABIOLA re-opens the door.*

FABIOLA *(CONT'D)*: Sebastián. It is me!

SEBASTIÁN: Fabiola?

FABIOLA: Pilar?

PILAR: Mami?

FABIOLA: Sebastián!

SEBASTIÁN: Fabiola?

FABIOLA: What are the two of you doing here?

> *More heightened music.*

FABIOLA *(CONT'D)*: So this is the innocent girl you met earlier!

SEBASTIÁN: I destroy everything I touch.

FABIOLA: You have both betrayed me!

PILAR: Wait. Mami why are you here? With a suitcase?

FABIOLA: For you of course, my wayward daughter. Your father is throwing you out...and I wanted you to have your things...to give you as much help as possible.

PILAR: Mami, this suitcase is not for me.

PILAR grabs the suitcase. It opens. Money and jewels, lingerie come tumbling out.

FABIOLA: See?

(She starts stuffing money in PILAR's pockets.)

I am giving you all the money I have tucked away, so you can survive until your father forgives you.

PILAR: *(Holds up the fancy slinky gown or lingerie.)* No. You are here for him.

FABIOLA: What are you saying?

PILAR: You are here to run away with Sebastián!

FABIOLA: Pilar, stop saying crazy things!

*ACTOR *(HORTENCIA)*: In the US, 60% of daughters describe their relationship with their mothers as "strained… and dysfunctional."

PILAR: Sebastián, have you slept with my mother?

FABIOLA: Do not answer her question, Sebastián!

SEBASTIÁN: Yes.

PILAR: *(Screams.)* No!

SEBASTIÁN: Pilar, it was something we should never have started but it is over now.

PILAR: Stop! I am filth, and *(To FABIOLA.)* You are filth, and you, Sebastián, are a STEP-MOTHER FUCKER!

PILAR runs out of the room. FABIOLA turns around and slaps SEBASTIÁN.

SEBASTIAN: PILAR!

FABIOLA: I could kill you.

SEBASTIÁN: Loving my sister is a fate worse than death.

FABIOLA: One night with her, and you are consumed? Why could you not love me that way?

SEBASTIÁN: The heart wants what the heart wants.

FABIOLA: And all I ever wanted was you.

FABIOLA starts to cry.

Why is fate so cruel? I marry the father, and I fall in love with the son, who falls for the daughter.

SEBASTIÁN: The daughter who is his half–sister. Oh God, what is to become of me?

ACTORS at the edge of their seats, barely dare to breathe.

FABIOLA: There is no worse sin.

SEBASTIÁN: I know. She is the first woman I have ever truly loved.

FABIOLA: Why her?

SEBASTIÁN: In her eyes, I could see our destiny. In her heart, I could feel the pulse of hope. Now I have destroyed it all.

FABIOLA: Sebastián, could you ever love me like her?

SEBASTIÁN: No.

FABIOLA: No…

FABIOLA pulls a small stiletto knife from her bra. Suddenly she stabs him in the back and side. Rose petals like blood come out of his wound. SEBASTIÁN falls dead.

Oh God, how I loved you. Why did it have to end this way, Sebastián?

*Forlorn FABIOLA drapes herself on SEBASTIÁN's dead body.
ARMANDO walks in.*

ARMANDO: Fabiola?

FABIOLA: Armando!

ARMANDO: What are you doing here?

FABIOLA: Looking for our daughter. What are you doing here?

ARMANDO: I was waiting in the lobby for Sebastián. We are searching for Pilar.

FABIOLA: Oh Armando! Something terrible has happened!

ARMANDO: *(He sees the body.)* Sebastián. He is bleeding!

FABIOLA: I am so sorry, Armando.

ARMANDO: What have you done, Fabiola?

FABIOLA: Me?

She drops the bloody knife in her hand.

I did nothing. It was Pilar Esperanza.

ARMANDO: Pilar did this?

FABIOLA: She stabbed Sebastián. And then ran off into the night.

ARMANDO: My daughter killed my son. Why?

FABIOLA: Pilar did not want to share you or her inheritance with him.

ARMANDO: First I catch her in the arms of another woman and then she stabs her brother…? The devil has gotten into our daughter!

FABIOLA: This is all your fault! You indulged her poetry and turned Pilar into a dangerous pervert. I told you not to hire that degenerate maid Victoria Maria but you did!

ARMANDO: Oh God, what have I done?

FABIOLA: Your son's death is all your fault, Armando.

FABIOLA dives on her suitcase to gather her stuff.

ARMANDO: Sebastián, why did I ever throw you out? God, forgive me. Now I have lost both my children. Wait. Wait! He is breathing. He is still breathing.

FABIOLA: He is? That cannot be.

ARMANDO: Help me, Fabiola, help me. We must get him to the hospital. My daughter might be dead to me...but my son is still alive!

ARMANDO starts to exit. FABIOLA looks at the suitcase and grabs it with her free arm and pulls it out of the room while helping ARMANDO pick up SEBASTIÁN.

SCENE 5: SERVANTS, POETS, AND DAUGHTERS

ACTOR(VICTORIA): (With placard:) Servants, poets, and daughters.

COP 2 (DR. DIEGO) brings in the prison – COP (former DR. MENDOZA) comes in dragging an angry weepy PILAR.

COP: Look who we have here! Some crazy girl. She was found wandering in the streets calling out someone's name! Disorderly conduct. Resisting arrest...

PILAR: I need to find my friend! Stop touching me!

COP: Why is that a problem, whore?

HORTENCIA: Never call a woman that. We are all someone's daughter. Or sister or mother.

COP: I am sorry. You are right.

COP exits.

HORTENCIA: *(Beat.)* Child, are you all right? You are Pilar Esperanza Josefina Castillo.

PILAR: *(Beat.)* Hortencia?

HORTENCIA: What are you doing here?

PILAR: *(Starts to cry.)* Oh Hortencia,

She falls to the floor.

HORTENCIA: My poor little girl. What has happened to you?

PILAR: I am a terrible person. Everything about me, is wrong.

HORTENCIA: Please do not say things like that. It breaks my heart.

She strokes PILAR's hair.

PILAR: I am filth. I am degenerate. I am bad. I am despicable.

HORTENCIA: No.

PILAR: I am worthless.

HORTENCIA: No.

PILAR: I deserve to die.

HORTENCIA: No.

PILAR: I want to die.

HORTENCIA starts to sing her song.

PILAR'S LULLABY

HORTENCIA: WAKE UP
OPEN YOUR EYES
WAKE UP
THERE'S NO TIME FOR LULLABIES
WAKE UP
SOON THE SUN WILL RISE
AND THERE CAN BE NO TOMORROW
WITHOUT YOU
YOUR SMILE IS LIKE THE MORNING STAR
YOU'RE THE LIGHT THAT BREAKS THE DAWN
YOU'RE THE FLAME THAT BURNS WITH LIFE,
MY CHILD
WAKE UP
WAKE UP
MY CHILD
WAKE UP

I know you. You are smart. You are sensitive. You are alone. And I was so much like you when I was young.

PILAR: Were you lonely too?

HORTENCIA: Smart women are always aware enough to be lonely. I am a woman who has worked for others every day of my life. Today I am in jail. I have not seen my husband and I do not know where he is… And my daughter has forsaken her dreams.

PILAR: I met your daughter…

HORTENCIA: Victoria Maria.

PILAR: Victoria Maria. She is like a friend I have known forever. Why did you never bring her to the house before?

HORTENCIA: Your mother would not allow it. She was worried that Victoria Maria would long for all the beautiful things you have.

PILAR: Victoria is not like that.

HORTENCIA: And sometimes I worried that Victoria might feel hurt by how much time I spend with you.

PILAR: She is your daughter. Blood of your blood.

HORTENCIA: I raised you too, my love.

PILAR: Hortencia, I have done something terrible with your daughter. And I pray you can forgive me.

Pause.

HORTENCIA: Pilar, what did you do?

PILAR: Victoria and I played a game.

HORTENCIA: What kind of game?

PILAR: A kissing game. Between the two of us.

HORTENCIA: Oh…that…

PILAR: I was impulsive. Please, forgive me.

HORTENCIA: For caring about my daughter? That is no crime.

PILAR: It feels like it is.

HORTENCIA: Nonsense. Many a girl's first kiss is with someone she loves and trusts.

PILAR: My father found us together. And he was furious.

HORTENCIA: Your father fears women who defy his control.

PILAR: I have never seen him so angry. He attacked us! He sent Victoria out into the storm/

HORTENCIA: Oh my God! Is she alright? Where is she?/

PILAR: /I have been looking for her.

HORTENCIA: /Did you find her?

PILAR: Oh Hortencia. It is all my fault.

HORTENCIA: You are not to blame, Pilar.

PILAR: We need to get out of here!

HORTENCIA: Guard! Guard!

PILAR: Hortencia, there is something else I need to tell you…

HORTENCIA: What is it? Guard!

PILAR: Sebastián…

HORTENCIA: What about your brother?

PILAR: We…we

HORTENCIA: GUARD!

Suddenly the COP (DR. MENDOZA) returns with SISTER SONIA, interrupting.

COP: A nun has come to see you.

HORTENCIA: Sister Sonia! What are you doing here?

SISTER SONIA: I have brought a statement from the late Doctor Mendoza.

COP *(THE FORMER DR. MENDOZA)*: God rest his soul.

SISTER SONIA: He refuses to press charges against you or anyone. Dr. Jorge Ramiro Mendoza says he pulled the trigger.

HORTENCIA: My God! Is this true?

SISTER SONIA: *(Revealing DOCTOR MENDOZA's statement with a flourish.)* I have his signed statement right here.

HORTENCIA: What does this mean?

SISTER SONIA: It means you are free to go, Hortencia. Guard, release the prisoner.

COP: Yes, sister!

The COP opens the jail cell and HORTENCIA steps out. Then HORTENCIA looks back at PILAR.

HORTENCIA: And what about her?

COP: She stays.

HORTENCIA: No, she does not. She is the daughter of Armando Castillo!

COP: She said she was your daughter, Victoria Maria.

PILAR: I did. I did not want my father to find me.

SISTER SONIA: Officer, this girl is known throughout Bellarica as the daughter of Armando Castillo.

COP: She looks like her. You are lying!

PILAR: I am Pilar Esperanza, daughter of Armando Castillo

This woman is my maid.

PILAR bribes COP.

COP: Then get her out of here.

HORTENCIA: We must find my daughter! Hurry, Pilar!

PILAR and HORTENCIA exit.

COP: But if I find out that she is not who you say she is…

SISTER SONIA: Señor, the truth is, only God knows who anyone truly is.

COP exits.

It is another rainy and stormy night. Here at the hospital!

ACTOR (PILAR): (With placard:) Life, Destiny, and Denouement.

SCENE 6: LIFE, DESTINY, AND DENOUEMENT

The hospital. SISTER SONIA pivots and she is back in the hospital. ARMANDO and FABIOLA enter carrying a dead-like unconscious SEBASTIÁN... FABIOLA is also pulling the suitcase.

ARMANDO: Sister Sonia! Sister Sonia!

FABIOLA: Help us!

SISTER SONIA: What a night! Look at this poor young man...

ARMANDO: Where is Doctor Mendoza?

SISTER SONIA: Dr. Mendoza is dead. And his son, Dr. Diego Mendoza...is in surgery.

ARMANDO: I need help with my son!

FABIOLA: He is bleeding from a knife wound. His sister stabbed him in the back.

HORTENCIA and PILAR burst in.

PILAR: We need to find Victoria del Rio.

HORTENCIA: Is she here?

ARMANDO:	PILAR:
Pilar!	Father!

PILAR *(CONT'D)*: Wait—is this Sebastián?

ARMANDO: You did this to him! Your own brother!

PILAR: Brother…what happened? Answer me. Who did this to you?

SISTER SONIA starts to tend to him.

SISTER SONIA: Put pressure there.

ARMANDO: Yes.

SISTER SONIA: More pressure. Good. Wipe his brow.

PILAR: Like this?

SISTER SONIA: Yes. Gently.

ARMANDO: What more can I do?

SISTER SONIA: Comfort him. What did you sing to him when he was a baby?

ARMANDO: I never sang to him. His mother, Sofia did…

DUERMETE MI NIÑO
DUERMETE MI SOL

ARMANDO stops. SISTER SONIA helps him finish.

WITH SISTER SONIA AND HORTENCIA: DUERMETE
PEDAZO DE MI CORAZÓN

SISTER SONIA: That is the song I used to sing to my son… Sebastián.

Everyone looks.

The boat… Your affair.

ARMANDO: Sister Sonia?

SISTER SONIA: We had a fight. I fell into the water.

ARMANDO: What are you saying?

SISTER SONIA: I remember it all!

FABIOLA: She is insane!

SISTER SONIA: I am not crazy.

Takes off her habit and reveals a stunning dress.

I am Sofia Milagro de Castillo!

ARMANDO: Sofia! I thought you were dead.

SISTER SONIA: The nuns found me, on the beach, without a name, without a past and they took me in.

ARMANDO: My God! Amnesia for twenty years!

FABIOLA: Armando, you really did push your first wife overboard?

ARMANDO: No!

SISTER SONIA: Yes!

ARMANDO: No! It was an accident. You tripped. You fell. You disappeared in the dark water. You drowned. You were dead.

SISTER SONIA: I have been here all this time. Doing something good with my life.

FABIOLA: You are unrecognizable!

SISTER SONIA: No! People overlook women of a certain age. But I am back. And now I have to save our son. The knife did not go deep, but he lost a lot of blood.

ARMANDO: Pilar, you stabbed your brother.

PILAR: Papi, I did not do this! When I left him he was alive and alone with: my mother.

All look to FABIOLA

FABIOLA: Armando, it was self–defense.

ARMANDO: What are you saying, Fabiola?

FABIOLA: Your children are liars and thieves. They want to steal your great fortune and to destroy the Castillo name. Everything I did, I did for you.

ARMANDO: My God! Fabiola!

ERNESTO enters.

ERNESTO: HORTENCIA!

HORTENCIA: Ernesto!

He rushes to her and hugs her.

Where is Victoria Maria?

ERNESTO: She is in surgery.

HORTENCIA: Oh my God. What happened to her?

ERNESTO: She is finally getting a healthy heart.

HORTENCIA: What?

SISTER SONIA: You were right. Victoria needed a heart transplant all these years. And somehow…

ERNESTO: Somehow…

SISTER SONIA: The Lord finally provided.

HORTENCIA: After all these years! I cannot believe it! A miracle! Whose heart is it?

DOCTOR DIEGO pushes in an unconscious VICTORIA. Wind blows. The world is taking on its own magic…

DOCTOR DIEGO: My father's heart.

Everyone turns.

HORTENCIA: Dr. Mendoza is the donor? How could you put that man's heart into my daughter's body?

DOCTOR DIEGO: My father has finally done his duty as a doctor. He is healing her. His heart is helping her live.

PILAR: She is going to live! Oh Victoria Maria!

VICTORIA: Pilar?

VICTORIA gets out of bed and hugs her best friend.

PILAR: I am here, Victoria. Your friend, always.

VICTORIA: And I yours. Papi… Mami! Am I dreaming?

HORTENCIA: No my love. I am out of jail.

ERNESTO: We are a family once more.

DOCTOR DIEGO: Victoria Maria, you have defied all the odds.

VICTORIA: I have done it all my life.

DOCTOR DIEGO: It is remarkable how well you are responding to the surgery.

VICTORIA: Doctor, thank you for my new heart.

DOCTOR DIEGO: And I hope one day, your new heart will find its way to loving me like I love you.

VICTORIA: *(Very softly.)* But I do love you, Doctor Diego.

DOCTOR DIEGO: *(Pulls out a box with a ring.)* Victoria, will you marry me?

VICTORIA: Yes. Yes. Yes!

VICTORIA and DOCTOR DIEGO embrace.

ERNESTO:	HORTENCIA:
No. No. No.	No. No. No.

ERNESTO: She must go to the University!

HORTENCIA: She must follow her dreams!

VICTORIA: I will study, Mami. Dr. Diego will help me. I will be a cardiologist. Together we will both be doctors and open a free clinic for the poor. This is my dream.

DOCTOR DIEGO: We have the same dream! I am the luckiest man on earth.

PILAR holds hands with unconscious bedridden SEBASTIÁN.

SEBASTIÁN: Pilar…

SISTER SONIA: My son is waking.

SEBASTIÁN: Mother?

SISTER SONIA: Son!

SEBASTIÁN: Sister.

PILAR: Brother. It is me, Pilar.

SEBASTIÁN: Oh Pilar, God forgive us both.

PILAR: I am your sister, Sebastián. But I love you.

SEBASTIÁN: I love you too. But our love can never be.

ARMANDO: My daughter loves my son? My son loves my daughter? My first wife is not dead? My God, what is happening?

SISTER SONIA: Armando Castillo, this beautiful child is not your daughter.

Looks all around.

FABIOLA: Of course she is. She is OUR daughter.

ARMANDO: Yes. I was here at the hospital…

SISTER SONIA: Yes. And so was Hortencia.

FABIOLA: Shut up, Sofia.

SISTER SONIA: It was a rainy and stormy night. Hortencia and Ernesto del Rio came in and she gave birth to a beautiful healthy baby girl.

HORTENCIA: But she got sick–

SISTER SONIA: No, she got switched.

Looks all around.

Fabiola Castillo's sweet baby girl was born sick. Fabiola decided to switch them. She raised Hortencia and Ernesto's child.

PILAR: What?

ERNESTO: And you helped them?

SISTER SONIA: The sickly child would have never survived with Fabiola.

HORTENCIA: Wait! Is that why Dr. Mendoza insisted we could never donate blood for her operations?

DOCTOR DIEGO: Victoria is one of the rarest blood types: AB Negative.

ARMANDO: My God. Like me. Her blood is my blood. Victoria is my daughter.

SEBASTIÁN: Is that true? Pilar, is not my sister? You are not my sister?

PILAR and SEBASTIÁN kiss like crazy. FABIOLA tries to slink away with the suitcase.

PILAR: Oh, Sebastián. I love you.

SEBASTIÁN: I love you too.

SISTER SONIA: Dr. Mendoza orchestrated the whole thing. For years.

DOCTOR DIEGO: How could my father do this terrible thing?

SISTER SONIA: The prestige and money seduced him. And I was his silent accomplice. But all of it was planned by one person. Fabiola Castillo.

Light on an quietly tip-toeing/escaping FABIOLA.

PILAR: Call the police.

FABIOLA: I would not call the police if I were you, Pilar. Not if you love your "friend", Victoria Maria.

PILAR: What do you mean?

FABIOLA: It was Victoria Maria who shot Doctor Mendoza for his heart!

DOCTOR DIEGO: Victoria, is that true?

VICTORIA: It was an accident.

HORTENCIA: I shot him.

ERNESTO: I am the one that killed the Doctor!

FABIOLA: You poor people! Looks like you and your entire family will rot in jail, Hortencia.

FABIOLA takes off her earrings and tries to start a fight. HORTENCIA does not budge or fight. HORTENCIA blocks her, takes off FABIOLA's wig; stripping her of her vanity. Everyone gasps.

SISTER SONIA: There is only one person to blame for Doctor Mendoza's death. Himself.

DR. DIEGO: My father made some bad decisions.

PILAR: Hortencia, is my mother. Armando is your father.

ARMANDO: This changes everything.

VICTORIA: My parents will always be Hortencia and Ernesto. Not you.

ARMANDO: I will try to be a better father, one that you deserve. You are my family.

ERNESTO: The truth is Armando, that we are all one family. Pilar Esperanza is my child! And Victoria Maria is my niece.

HORTENCIA, FABIOLA: What?

ARMANDO, SEBASTIÁN, DOCTOR DIEGO: What?

PILAR AND VICTORIA: What?

MUSICIAN: What?

ERNESTO: Fabiola is not the daughter of a wealthy ranch owner.

FABIOLA: Shut up, Ernesto!

ERNESTO: Fabiola is my sister!

VICTORIA AND PILAR: We are cousins?

ERNESTO: *(Looks at the audience.)* You are kissing cousins.

ARMANDO: Fabiola, our whole life together was built on lies.

FABIOLA: I had to pretend. The perfect woman you wanted as a wife, Armando, does not exist...anywhere. So I became what men wanted to see. I am a woman in a man's world. And to succeed, to survive, I learned to be ruthless and to play the game of life by the same rules as greedy men.

PILAR: How's that working out for you, Mami?

FABIOLA: Meh.

ARMANDO: Sofia, take me back. You are still my wife.

FABIOLA: I am still your wife.

SISTER SONIA: No. I am very happy with the sisters in the convent. But as to the Castillo Fortune…

ARMANDO AND FABIOLA: Yes…?

SISTER SONIA: The Milagro Casino is mine. When I disappeared, you changed the casino's name, but you could not change her destiny. I am giving my casino to Sebastián and Pilar. The profits will help build a free clinic for Dr. Diego and Victoria.

FABIOLA: No! Our fortune?

ARMANDO: Gone! Gone!

SISTER SONIA: Armando, I can find you a job…as a doorman.

FABIOLA: And what about me?

Sirens come. The POLICE come in.

POLICE *(FORMER DR. MENDOZA)*: Police.

SISTER SONIA: For the attempted murder of my son.

FABIOLA: No!

FABIOLA, in one heel, tries to limp out with some dignity.

SISTER SONIA: Fabiola, justice will prevail.

FABIOLA: My suitcase. I need my suitcase.

SISTER SONIA: Fabiola, the suitcase stays!

FABIOLA: My wig. I need my wig.

(Gets it.) If you think I am spending one night in jail, you are sadly mistaken. I am Fabiola Castillo.

*ACTOR *(FABIOLA)*: The Telenovela is the number one form of entertainment in the world today. Over two billion people, one third of the human race, watch these stories every night.

SISTER SONIA: Armando, open the door for your wife. It will be good practice for your new job.

FABIOLA and ARMANDO exit.

ARMANDO: Yes, Sister.

SEBASTIÁN: I renounce the Castillo name. I will now be Sebastián Jose Milagro.

PILAR: I am no longer a Castillo. I am free.

SEBASTIÁN: *(Pulls out a ring box with an engagement ring.)* Pilar Esperanza, marry me!

PILAR: But I must have time every day to write. I will go to the University. I want a masters, no! A PhD! I want access to affordable birth control and equal pay. And if we choose to have children, we will raise our sons to respect women. And our daughters to change the world. Do you agree?

SEBASTIÁN: I do.

PILAR: Let us marry.

DOCTOR DIEGO: Yes!

VICTORIA AND PILAR: Yes!

PILAR: Call the Priest!

VICTORIA: Where is the Priest?

Beat.

HORTENCIA: Sister, you should marry them–

SISTER SONIA: Me?

HORTENCIA: Why not?

Hospital curtains become gorgeous veils. The girls become brides.

The couples prepare for the wedding.

EL DESTINO DEL DESEO

ALL: *(Sung slowly.)* EL DESTINO DEL DESEO
EL DESEO DEL DESTINO
ME CONSUMEN COMO EL FUEGO
Y TU AMOR ES EL CAMINO
EL DESTINO DEL DESEO
EL DESEO DEL DESTINO
ME CONSUMEN COMO EL FUEGO
Y TU AMOR ES EL CAMINO

SISTER SONIA. Who here will witness this wedding?

HORTENCIA, ERNESTO: We will.

HORTENCIA and ERNESTO escort the girls.

VICTORIA and DOCTOR DIEGO and SEBASTIÁN and PILAR before SISTER SONIA.

SISTER SONIA: We are gathered here to join these young souls in blessed matrimony.

Sebastián and Dr. Diego, you take the woman before you as your lawful wedded wife?

SEBASTIÁN AND DOCTOR DIEGO: We do.

SISTER SONIA: And Victoria and Pilar do you accept these men as your lawfully wedded husbands?

VICTORIA AND PILAR: We do.

SISTER SONIA: I declare you married. Now Kiss!

PILAR AND VICTORIA: Like this?

PILAR and VICTORIA practice their telenovela kiss on the boys. SEBASTIÁN and PILAR kiss. VICTORIA and DOCTOR DIEGO kiss.

Then ever so slowly…

VICTORIA and PILAR sexily hook pinkies as they kiss their husbands…

*ACTOR *(FABIOLA)*: The End.

SONG: THE DESTINY OF DESIRE

THE FULL ENSEMBLE:

SINGS ROUSING CHORUS

EL DESTINO DEL DESEO
EL DESEO DEL DESTINO
ME CONSUMEN COMO EL FUEGO
Y TU AMOR ES EL CAMINO
EL DESTINO DEL DESEO
EL DESEO DEL DESTINO
ME CONSUMEN COMO EL FUEGO
Y TU AMOR ES EL CAMINO

Celebration! BUBBLES.

END OF PLAY.

FOOTNOTES FOR FACTS ACT 1

At hospitals in the United States, about one in eight babies is given to the wrong mother. Temporarily or permanently https://brandongaille.com/20-babies-switched-at-birth-statistics/

Chance Encounters in the United States have a 25% higher rate of failure than on–line dating.
http://www3.nd.edu/~ghaeffel/OnineDating_Aron.pdf
http://www.yourtango.com/experts/author–blue–sullivan/truth–about–online–dating

Last year, 285 children under the age of eighteen picked up a firearm and accidentally shot themselves or someone else.
https://www.washingtonpost.com/news/wonk/wp/2015/12/31/kids-accidentally-shot-people-5-times-a-week-this-year-on-average/?utm_term=.f78b38fc4213

The United States imprisons more people that any other nation in the world. About one out of every one hundred Americans is in prison.
https://www.washingtonpost.com/news/fact-checker/wp/2015/07/07/yes-u-s-locks-people-up-at-a-higher-rate-than-any-other-country/?utm_term=.6bb6bbf2c0e2

In the United States, women make up nearly two thirds of the minimum wage workforce and more than half of them experience sexual harassment at work.
http://www.nwlc.org/resource/women–and–minimum–wage–state–state

Latinos in the United States have a higher life expectancy than white or black Americans despite lower wages and poor access to healthcare. This is called the Hispanic Paradox.
http://www.bbc.com/news/world–us–canada–32910129

68% of married women in the United States say they would have an affair if they knew they would never get caught. Oregon is in the United States. https://www.atlantapsych.com/article/affairs

Peer pressure increases risky behavior among adolescents. https://secure.uwf.edu/smathews/documents/peerroleinrisktakinggardnerandsteinberg.pdf

Statistically, women begin gambling later than men, but develop problems and addiction more quickly. http://knowtheodds.org/blog/women–problem–gambling–the–hidden–addiction/

56% of girls have kissed another girl…And liked it. https://www.psychologytoday.com/blog/power–and–prejudice/201207/girls–kissing–girls–0

ACT II

One person is found dead each day in the desert between in the United States and Mexico. http://www.aljazeera.com/indepth/features/2015/03/identifying–mexico–dead–border–150309063920308.html

Mexico is the largest Spanish speaking country in the world. The United States is the first. http://www.theguardian.com/us–news/2015/jun/29/us–second–biggest–spanish–speaking–country

On average, twenty-two people die each day waiting for a transplant. One donor could save eight lives. http://www.americantransplantfoundation.org/about–transplant/facts–and–myths/

60% of daughters describe their relationship with their

mothers as "strained… and dysfunctional."
http://www.medicalnewstoday.com/releases/149047.php
https://www.psychologytoday.com/blog/tech-
support/201502/8-types-toxic-patterns-in-mother-
daughter-relationships
http://www.webmd.com/balance/features/why-mothers-
daughters-cant-just-get-along

The Telenovela is the number one form of entertainment in
the world today. Some say that over 2 billion people, one
third of the human race, watch these stories every night.
http://news.bbc.co.uk/2/hi/americas/4842220.stm How
telenovelas conquered the world

NATIVE GARDENS

Native Gardens was commissioned and first produced by
Cincinnati Playhouse in the Park under

Blake Robison (Artistic Director) and
Buzz Ward (Managing Director).

Characters

TANIA DEL VALLE – 30 years old – smart, likeable, positive, passionate, fit and highly energized pregnant PhD candidate and gardener.

PABLO DEL VALLE – 32 years old – smart, likeable, ambitious, savvy young attorney.

VIRGINIA BUTLEY – 60-75 years old – smart, likeable, assertive, direct, no-nonsense engineer.

FRANK BUTLEY – 60-75 years old – smart, likeable, excitable, caring, detail-oriented federal employee and gardener.

The play should also use 2-4 extras to play the silent roles of the surveyor, landscapers, building examiner. There are short theatrical vignettes between scenes that can help transform the garden. These workers should preferably be Latinx and exude unique personalities as they work.

Setting

The back of two houses. Two back gardens. A wire fence with ivy divides them. One garden is a beautiful garden with lush grass and very symmetrical garden beds. The other is unkempt: dying hydrangeas… crab grass, a large oak tree, leaves, and acorns.

"The difference between a flower
and a weed…is a judgment"
-Unknown

Prologue - Spotlights

PABLO: First impressions are really– good.

TANIA: Great actually!

FRANK: Neighbors.

VIRGINIA: Not friends but friendly.

TANIA: Very neighborly.

FRANK: Tania and… Pablo are new to the neighborhood.

VIRGINIA: We welcome them by bringing over wine.

They look over at TANIA and PABLO.

FRANK: My guess is they prefer red wine over white.

PABLO: They give us Merlot and dark chocolate.

VIRGINIA: Chocolate is always… safe.

TANIA: I'm allergic, but it's so nice.

FRANK: So happy to get a young family on the street.

TANIA: An old home.

PABLO: A historic neighborhood!

VIRGINIA: Stately houses and gardens.

PABLO: Ours is a fixer-upper.

TANIA: With a fabulous back yard!

Everyone looks at the backyard.

And a tree!

PABLO: A tree.

FRANK: A tree.

VIRGINIA: A tree.

TANIA: A tree! Oh! I have big plans for this yard!

VIRGINIA AND FRANK: Old neighborhood.

TANIA AND PABLO: New neighbors.

FIRST VIGNETTE - MONDAY AFTERNOON

Music.

PABLO, FRANK and VIRGINIA exit. TANIA, almost eight months pregnant, still energized and nimble, is wearing comfortable clothes. She is trying to dig out a wilted plant. She is happy. Singing maybe, as she plays with the dirt. Her husband PABLO enters into the back yard. He is meticulously dressed in a nice suit.

SCENE 1- MONDAY AFTERNOON

PABLO: Tania! There you are!

TANIA: Pablo, you're home early.

PABLO: Should you be doing that?

TANIA: It's fine. I'm so sick of unpacking. I hate being inside on such a beautiful day!

PABLO: You should take it easy.

TANIA: Gardening relaxes me. You're the one that's been working so hard.

PABLO: I have to. This firm is so intense... So intensely ...

TANIA: Competitive?

PABLO: –American.

TANIA: American …

PABLO: American.

TANIA: You're just the new guy.

PABLO: No. I'm the foreign guy. And that's different.

TANIA: That's why they want you, because you are different.

PABLO: Tania, I think I've done something I might regret.

TANIA: Really? What?

PABLO: I invited the entire firm to our house.

TANIA: You did what?

PABLO: The senior partners were joking about me being the "new guy." And Mr. Krause, as in SMITH, KRAUSE and WILSON, said he barely thinks you exist–

TANIA: –But, you told him I'm finishing my dissertation… and the baby– right?

PABLO: Before I knew it, I channeled my father and invited all of them over to our house.

TANIA: You didn't!

PABLO: It gets better: the party is this weekend.

TANIA: Puta madre!!!

PABLO: Breathe. Breathe. Remember the Lamaze …

TANIA: Maldita sea. Are you crazy!? How did that happen?

PABLO: I'll tell you how: the letterhead partner, Mr. Krause, says "Pablo! That's a generous offer. When would you like us ALL over?" And I say, "Sir, mi casa es su casa" And we all laugh. And he says, "I'd love to see where you live. Tell you what, I'm free this Saturday."

TANIA: Saturday! –

PABLO: –"Does that work for you?" It was a test. A total test. He was watching me with this gleam in his eye.

TANIA: This is where you say NO… it doesn't work for me or my beloved pregnant wife!

PABLO: I didn't skip a beat. Looked him straight in the eye and said: YES! Mr. Krause, this Saturday is perfect. And he said: "I like that. You have cojones, son."

TANIA: Mr. Krause actually said "cojones?"

PABLO: He even did the quotation marks.

TANIA: Oh God.

PABLO: I see it as his form of cultural outreach. Which could be a good sign to becoming partner.

TANIA: No! Nothing about this ballsy, machista law firm party-planning is good!

PABLO: I know. But Tania: this could be bigger than Steven Johnsons' Martini Happy Hour. Because the only living, letterhead boss said he would come. I could become the first Latino to make partner in this place. Maybe one day, they'll add DEL VALLE to the letterhead. That would be a first, huh?

TANIA: Pablo!

PABLO: It was fight or flight, Tania. And you've taught me to never run away from a fight.

TANIA: Sixty strangers here in six days? We don't have enough furniture. Our walls are half painted. Our plaster is cracked. And I have my own research to do before the baby comes. It's just too much. You are trying too hard.

PABLO: I know! I know. It's too much. I'm so stressed. I don't want to let you down. I don't want to let the baby down. I want to fix up the house for us. I need to make partner –

TANIA: So an impromptu party for the whole firm?

PABLO: I don't know what I was thinking. We can't fix-up a fixer-upper in six days… I'll tell Mr. Krause that I can't deliver.

TANIA: Wait! So let's be upfront, confident. Show them we are do-it-yourselfers in the best way: we have the party outside.

PABLO: Outside.

TANIA: In this beautiful yard. With our gorgeous tree.

PABLO: Tania, our yard is not beautiful.

TANIA: Not yet. But it can be.

PABLO: Your Native Garden.

TANIA: I've had the design in my head since we bought the place. If we pull away some of that patched grass… get rid of those plants and that gnome and allow those there to get some light. Plant some ferns, bushes and wildflowers. Add some filtered water in the bird bath. And the oak looks so majestic. Oh my God, this could be very exciting.

PABLO: But we agreed to fix the house first and then you could start thinking of the garden.

TANIA: Pablo, do you want your party or not?

PABLO: I was thinking barbeque.

TANIA: Yeah!

PABLO: Americans love "B-B-Q". It puts everyone at ease. Cool and casual. Show them we comfortably fit in the landscape that they know. We can do American WASP success… or at least imitate it…

TANIA: Effortless looking effort.

PABLO: They will love my scholarly and vibrant wife. They will see this fine historic neighborhood and the potential of this unfinished place and say "Here is a man that understands smart risk. *(Maybe he grabs the rake and stands next to TANIA à la 'American Gothic'.)* He is the American Dream– incarnate."

TANIA: And maybe we can get someone to pull out that ugly sagging chain link fence. It's horrible.

PABLO: And put up the kind of stately wood fence a law firm would appreciate.

TANIA: We make sure people relax and open up. We win them over.

PABLO: You are incredible. Thank you.

TANIA: Don't thank me yet. We only have six days.

PABLO: Can we pull this off?

TANIA: First, we need to talk to the neighbors. Frank and Virginia need to be OK with us changing the fence.

PABLO: Who would fight us for changing this ugly fence?

TANIA: Their English ivy is draping the fence. And believe it or not …. people can get very weird about their plants.

SECOND VIGNETTE - MONDAY EVENING

Music. We see FRANK come out the back of his house with a bottle of pesticide. He sprays sections of the garden before VIRGINIA comes out and beckons him. All enter out to the deck, with TANIA and PABLO gifting VIRGINIA and FRANK a bottle of wine in a gift bag. FRANK goes inside to prepare it. TANIA and PABLO and VIRGINIA start the scene.

SCENE 2 - MONDAY EVENING

(TANIA and PABLO sit in VIRGINIA and FRANK's perfect garden. FRANK is off-stage.)

VIRGINIA: Well, we are so happy to finally have real homeowners living next door. It used to be such a beautiful place until Mr. Whitefield died and then Mrs. Whitefield died and her stupid stepson took over and rented it to a bunch of sloppy Georgetown students ... But now. A fresh start. And a baby! We love babies. Maybe we can babysit! Frank's bringing out wine glasses. Frank! Bring out some iced tea. For the little pregnant lady!

TANIA: We don't mean to bother you on a work night.

VIRGINIA: Nonsense, Frank does his consulting from home now. And I've been an engineer at Lockheed Martin so long, I have my own bathroom.

PABLO: At Lockheed Martin!

VIRGINIA: Yes, shocking huh?

PABLO: Oh no, not at all.

VIRGINIA: I bet some of your best friends are old female defense contractors. Right?

Laughs.

FRANK emerges with a tray carrying iced tea, wine glasses and the wine PABLO and TANIA brought over.

FRANK: So did you know that all the houses on this street were built in 1908?

PABLO AND TANIA: Really –

VIRGINIA: As were most of the residents!

Laughs.

I'm joshing. But it is an old neighborhood. Mr. and Mrs. Jenkins across the street were part of the Bush Jr. and Sr. administrations. And Phillip Saxon– in the blue house… the one with the great ornate front yard –

FRANK: –It's not that great –

VIRGINIA: I meant great as in big. Frank and Phillip have a gardening rivalry.

FRANK: Very friendly and neighborly, I assure you.

VIRGINIA: Every year awards are given by the Garden Club–

FRANK: Potomac Horticultural Society.

VIRGINIA: And Frank's garden always wins… honorable mention!

PABLO: It's beautiful. It reminds me of my parents' garden.

TANIA: Very European.

FRANK: Thank you. But Phillip Saxon has won Best Garden for the last three years.

VIRGINIA: Maybe not this year. I think you've outdone yourself.

FRANK: The Horticultural Society judges come by this Sunday.

TANIA: This Sunday?

PABLO: Oh no.

TANIA: We were coming over to talk about replacing the
fence.

FRANK: Replacing that fence?

TANIA: By Saturday… for an event we are having.

FRANK: Are you serious?

VIRGINIA: You want to replace the fence this week?

TANIA: I'm sorry. Pablo, this isn't going to work –

FRANK: Sorry? This is the best news I've heard in a while.

PABLO: It is?

FRANK: One day that stupid Whitefield stepson just put up
that cheap garish thing.

TANIA: Oh, so it's our fence?

VIRGINIA: It certainly isn't ours. Frank sicced the English ivy
on it so we would see green instead of chain link.

FRANK: English Ivy is potent if used de-fens-ively.

Laughter.

But no matter what I do, Phillip Saxon doesn't have to
contend with a disheveled wire fence.

TANIA: Well if you are OK about us cutting away your ivy,
we could get rid of the wire fence.

PABLO: And replace it with a tall, stately wood one.

FRANK: A Christmas miracle in September.

PABLO: I'm so relieved you are "on board" with this.

Laughter.

FRANK: I'm surprised how elated I am. I hate that fence.

PABLO: So do we.

FRANK: I hate losing to Phillip Saxon too!

VIRGINIA: Frank, calm down. The point of gardening is for you to relieve your chronic stress.

FRANK: It's not that bad.

VIRGINIA: Yeah, right.

Beat.

Anyway, it's so much better since he discovered he has a green thumb.

FRANK: It started with a bulb. I put it in the ground, and a tulip came up. And I was amazed by what I had done! It was like... childbirth.

VIRGINIA: *(To TANIA.)* Tulips are nothing like childbirth.

FRANK: Everything you see here, I planted with my own hands –

VIRGINIA: On his knees. Meticulously.

TANIA: Wow. Is it me or does your yard look bigger than our yard?

VIRGINIA: Bigger? No. More organized, perhaps.

PABLO: It's so neat. So pristine ...

FRANK: *(Laughs.)* Every day, I rake. I trim. I mow. I fertilize. I mulch. I de-grub. I spray for bugs.

TANIA: You use pesticides?

FRANK: Constantly!

VIRGINIA: And he constantly weeds. He see's something that's out of place and he grabs it by the roots and pulls it out. Immediately. It's a little OCD, but the results are impressive.

PABLO: Tania is an avid gardener too!

TANIA: My grandparents owned a small farm and I've always loved playing in the dirt. I'm so excited about owning a yard.

FRANK: I'm happy to help you become a serious garden contender.

TANIA: Oh, thank you, but your gardening might be too… ambitious for me.

VIRGINIA: She has a job and a little baby on the way.

FRANK: Well, gardener to gardener, the one thing you should get rid of is that tree …

PABLO: You mean, our oak?

VIRGINIA: You mean your future disaster!

Laughs.

TANIA: Disaster?

FRANK: It's so dangerous.

TANIA: But. We. Love. The tree.

PABLO: We do.

VIRGINIA: Really?

TANIA: Really.

FRANK: We used to have the sister oak in our back yard… but we decided to get rid of it. To safe guard our roof and give us a canvas on which to plant. One life for so many.

PABLO: You had an oak tree like ours here?

FRANK: And it completely overwhelmed our yard. Just like yours. Those heavy craggy branches up there need to be cut back which is expensive. I suggest just chopping the whole thing down as soon as possible.

VIRGINIA: How about right now? We have a chain saw. And an axe!

FRANK: Oh Ginny. You will need a professional tree guy, of course. Post-haste.

TANIA: It's a healthy tree. We had that inspected before we bought the house.

FRANK: But the tree is why your lawn looks so messy. All the leaves and acorns. Everywhere.

VIRGINIA: And we get your leaves and acorns. All over our lot.

TANIA: The tree is the centerpiece of our plan for a Native Garden.

FRANK: Native Garden? That sounds very exotic.

TANIA: Actually, it's very traditional. We want to go back to the basics, get rid of foreign plants like Bermuda grass, and English ivy, and nurture a native Mid-Atlantic forest bed.

PABLO: Which is better for the environment.

TANIA: Native plants feed the right bees and bugs, the right bugs feed the birds, and so on. We, the individual gardeners of America have the opportunity, or dare I say, the responsibility in helping ensure biodiversity in our gardens. We can help save the planet.

VIRGINIA: My. That's a patriotic call to action.

TANIA: I have some books. Written by brilliant entomologists. I can bring them to you.

FRANK: So… you are suggesting: No azalea? No peonies? No hydrangeas?

TANIA: No Japanese honeysuckle, no Asian azalea, no kudzu, no Bradford pear, no autumn olive.

FRANK: Blasphemy!

TANIA: But there are beautiful ferns, mulberry, Virginia creeper, Carolina silverbell. Low maintenance greenery that's high output and low impact.

FRANK: You mean, weeds? You are planting weeds, on purpose?

TANIA: A lot of plants we think of as weeds are actually native plants and they have a purpose.

VIRGINIA: Isn't it their purpose to be ugly?

Everyone Laughs.

TANIA: *(Good naturedly.)* That's a misconception. Native plants can be quite arresting.

FRANK: So, you are going to plant a bunch of weeds –

VIRGINIA: –So that your yard will attract more bees and bugs?

TANIA: Yes.

FRANK	VIRGINIA
Fascinating.	Crazy.

TANIA: Do you listen to NPR? National Public Radio?

VIRGINIA: Of course we listen to NPR.

FRANK: We're old, not dead.

TANIA: NPR had a great segment on native gardening. You should listen to it.

VIRGINIA: Are you all vegetarian?

TANIA: No –

PABLO: We love barbeque

FRANK: Is this Native Garden something that springs from your rich Mexican culture?

TANIA: It's a gardening philosophy developed by entomologists.

FRANK: It seems so rooted to a Mexican connection to the Earth. There must be something there.

TANIA: Except, we're not Mexican.

PABLO: I'm from Las Condes Santiago, Chile. I did Boarding school here.

TANIA: And, I'm from… New Mexico.

FRANK: Funny. I was sure I detected a little Spanish accent from you.

VIRGINIA: That's why we thought you were Mexican.

TANIA: That's so interesting because I'm American. I don't even speak very much Spanish.

PABLO: She can swear in Spanish.

TANIA: Maybe you imagined the accent?

VIRGINIA: Maybe, it's just that you look so Mexican.

TANIA AND PABLO: *(Smiling. Good natured.)* That's what people tell us.

VIRGINIA: *(Beat.)* We love Mexico. Love it.

FRANK: Saw the Pyramid of The Sun in Mexico City.

VIRGINIA: We saw Warren Beatty at a disco in Acapulco.

FRANK: No one talks about Acapulco anymore.

VIRGINIA: Mexico now is all Cancún, Cancún!

FRANK: And drug trafficking. Illegal immigration– and that wall business.

TANIA: I don't know Mexico very well.

FRANK: But you are Mexican-American, aren't you?

TANIA: In a sense, yes... but... Frank, where are your ancestors from?

FRANK: England. Mostly.

TANIA: Do you introduce yourself as English-American?

FRANK: Of course not. I'm a New Englander. From the North East

TANIA: See? I'm New Mexican. From the South West. But people think of me as much more foreign than you.

VIRGINIA: I on the other hand, am Polish-American. I like claiming the old country.

TANIA: My family has been in the same region for over two hundred years. Where I am from was originally part of Mexico, then it became part of the United States. We've been Americans for generations. We never immigrated. Yet because of how I look, my nationality is always in question.

PABLO: She is conducting some identity experiments. For her Doctoral dissertation in anthropology.

TANIA: I am interested in origins and when we claim them and when we stop. The power of language and place. Native vs. foreign. Especially in a country as complicated as the US.

PABLO: It's interesting and it's controversial.

FRANK: Hey! Our marriage was controversial in our day.

VIRGINIA: A wealthy New England blue blood and a blue collar Polish girl from Buffalo.

TANIA: This complexity is what makes us all... American.

PABLO: Actually, if we nitpick: You are Estado Unidense: United Statesean.

TANIA: True.

PABLO: Everyone in Canada, Latin America and the Caribbean is American.

FRANK: Oh c'mon, everyone refers to us as the Americans.

TANIA: That's true too!

PABLO: The English are Europeans –

FRANK: –Not anymore –

PABLO: The Australians are Australian. And all of us here are Americans. Except I'm Chilean. And you three are United Statesean.

Everyone laughs.

TANIA: Yes. So Pablo is the only foreigner here –

PABLO: Here and at my law firm.

VIRGINIA: Oh! My poor boy. Are you the token? And don't let anyone use that term. Because it's demeaning. I know. For twenty years, I was the only female engineer in my division, I was smarter than many of my colleagues, but because I didn't have a schlong to go along with my brain, or a really good baseball card collection, I was constantly tested, or being asked to get coffee, or-

FRANK: -interrupted-

VIRGINIA: *(Beat.)* and, Peter, Paul and Mary– the lady jokes. So many stupid "lady jokes." But I had the last laugh. I fought to get to where I am now. Are you fighting too?

PABLO	TANIA
Well…um…yes. But.	No, he's fine.

VIRGINIA: Be fierce and be fearless, amigo. Do everything you say you will and then, do more. We have to be twice as good to get half as far.

PABLO: Thank you.

VIRGINIA: And don't let those yahoos get you down.

PABLO: That's good advice.

VIRGINIA: More tea?

TANIA: I think I've had enough caffeine and sugar for one day, thank you.

VIRGINIA: You kids today are so cautious. When I was young, while other women were burning bras, I was wearing full support, working overtime. I couldn't let a thing like a child-birth slow me down. Drank coffee all night until my water broke. And our Scott is fine.

FRANK: He's a little quiet. Shy.

VIRGINIA: He works at the Library of Congress. He's a lovely boy.

FRANK: He's almost forty.

VIRGINIA: I hope he marries in this garden one day.

FRANK: I don't think so.

Beat.

PABLO: Oh my, look at the time. We have kept you out here … and the mosquitos.

VIRGINIA: Those darn bugs! And more to come …

TANIA: Spiders will help with the mosquitos. You'll see.

VIRGINIA: We will! Thank you for the wine.

FRANK: A pleasure talking with you.

TANIA: And thank you for allowing us to trim your ivy.

FRANK: Thank you for our new wood fence!

PABLO: What is that American saying: Good fences make good friends?

VIRGINIA: Good neighbors. Good fences make good neighbors.

FRANK: Amen.

VIGNETTE 3 - TUESDAY MORNING

VIRGINIA exits. FRANK crosses to the fence to grab his pesticide and finds an acorn. He looks around, then throws it in to the DEL VALLE yard – he exits. Lights shift; Tuesday morning. PABLO enters from his house, clothes not quite put together. He has a cup of coffee and the plat. He crosses to the fence, looking at the flowers on the other side

SCENE 3 - TUESDAY MORNING

TANIA enters with a pen and pad of paper.

TANIA: BBQ Jacks says they can bring eighteen pounds for Saturday. And the linens and tables and chairs will be set up that late morning.

PABLO: That's good. The first fence guy said it was impossible ... but then I found one that spoke Spanish...

TANIA: Viva la Raza!

PABLO: And he lowered the price, of course, for us.

TANIA: Membership has its privileges ...

PABLO: If we just give him a perimeter of the yard. He can get all the wood delivered by tomorrow, and installed by Friday.

TANIA. Friday! Perfect. Let me check it. Do you have the plans?

TANIA crosses to PABLO and takes the plat.

PABLO: The office is buzzing about our barbeque! Since Mr. Krause is coming... everyone is cancelling their plans to make sure they can come. Crazy as it sounds, this party might be one of the best impulse moves I've ever made.

TANIA: I'm just relieved about how happy the Butleys are about the new fence!

TANIA starts to study the perimeter.

PABLO: The Butleys are awesome. I love them.

TANIA: And they really "love" Mexico. *(Laughs.)*

PABLO: It was like we entered another time and place. Another galaxy...

241

TANIA: It's a live Dick Van Dyke Show… right next door.

PABLO: You think we'll be that out of touch when we're their age?

TANIA: No– because we are not white.

PABLO: But they're trying! They did offer to babysit!

TANIA: And I love them for that. Although, I didn't sense they approved of our approach to the garden.

PABLO: Maybe they thought we were being… judgemental?

TANIA: Me? I'm not being judgmental. Just informed.

PABLO: OK. You have to agree… what they have is beautiful.

TANIA: You can't mean that.

PABLO: OK. But it's pretty.

TANIA: Pretty evil! These "lovely" plants: bugs don't feed on them. Bees avoid them, causing crisis and chaos. Bees start to die. Birds move away. Butterflies fade. How is that beautiful?

PABLO: Is this a rally?

TANIA: The invasive Japanese honeysuckle is like the crack cocaine of the plant world. It should be illegal for nurseries to sell it.

PABLO: Operation Crack Down.

TANIA: This beautiful OAK tree is a banquet of nutrition and life. And I will not chop it down.

PABLO: Nobody said we would. Calm down.

TANIA: Don't tell me to calm down. It implies I'm being irrational… when I'm being passionately rational. Don't you like beautiful wildflowers?

PABLO: Sure. I guess. I just also– like those purple ones, and those white ones… those look –

TANIA: Whoa. Wait a second.

PABLO: What's the matter?

TANIA: Something here is not right.

PABLO: What?

TANIA: Well, it says here in the plan that our yard goes over to… That can't be

PABLO: Is there something wrong with the plan?

TANIA: Or something wrong with our yard. Look.

They both look at the plat and TANIA's notes.

PABLO: That is strange.

TANIA. I mean we would have to measure it.

PABLO: Why not? Where's the tape measure?

He crosses into the house to grab a measuring tape.

TANIA: Second junk drawer to the right.

PABLO: We have two junk drawers?

TANIA: Yes. We are very special people.

PABLO: Ah-ha! Aquí está!

Hands one end to TANIA.

TANIA: I'm sure it's nothing…

PABLO pulls out the tape and hands one end to TANIA. They measure the DS side of the yard – and come up short. They look over the fence, then at each other. TANIA shakes her head. PABLO

steps over to FRANK's garden, pulls the tape measure and looks at the tape measure.

PABLO: To here.

TANIA: No!!!!

PABLO: Yes! We own more than we think. Wow! Oh Wow!

TANIA: Get back over here. That can't be right.

PABLO: A que sí! It's what's filed at the city. This plan is what is attached to our mortgage. This is what we bought. This is the lot the stupid Whitefield stepson sold to us!

TANIA: But we didn't know that. We assumed our property went to the chain link fence.

PABLO: *(Running up and down excitedly.)* It's more: Two feet beyond: the flowerbeds, the ivy, the walkway. All the way to the street. It all belongs to us. To us! Huevón!!! We need to get a surveyor here as soon as possible.

TANIA: Oh no.

PABLO: *(Crosses back to their yard.)* You know what this means?

TANIA: Trouble?

PABLO: We may legally own 10% more yard than we thought.

TANIA: That much?

PABLO: God, I love the law!

VIGNETTE 4 - WEDNESDAY MORNING

The SURVEYOR comes in, with his/her measuring wheel and plat. He looks at the documents. Maybe FRANK enters with his gardening caddy. They wave at each other. FRANK exits in to the house. The SURVEYOR goes about his business, measuring along the edge of the yard... running right over FRANK's plants. He flags the flowerbed along the actual property line. TANIA enters a little stressed. The SURVEYOR hands her a bill and they exit. FRANK comes on, notices the flags, and does a little warm-up with his clippers as he crosses to the fence. He sits, and begins to clip away at the ivy. TANIA re-enters.

SCENE 4 - WEDNESDAY MORNING

(FRANK is cutting the English ivy. TANIA walks out.)

TANIA: Oh, Frank, that is so kind. I can clip the ivy. It's so much work.

FRANK: Only four more days until the judges. I can't rest now. Besides. I like work. I need it. Working with the earth "grounds me."

TANIA: Me too. And God knows when the little one comes, if I'll have the luxury to mess around back here.

FRANK: Babies and plants both love… nurseries!

TANIA: You're so punny.

FRANK: So was the fence man the guy measuring? He was in my yard, wasn't he? Those little flags… are his?

TANIA: That was the surveyor.

FRANK: Oh. It's so wise! You gotta call before you dig!

TANIA: Sure do!

She laughs nervously.

I have those books for you.

FRANK: "Bringing Nature Home." "Wild Urban Plants of the Northeast." "Insects are Essential." I can't wait.

TANIA: Not only is it great gardening; it's good reading.

FRANK: Thank you. So when are they coming to tear out the chain link fence?

TANIA: Tomorrow!

FRANK: And you ordered the wood fence?

TANIA: If all goes well, the entire fence will be in by Friday.
I'll be digging out here too.

FRANK: Maybe this year, with your new fence… I might win
the Potomac Horticultural Society Best Garden Award… a
man can dream, can't he?

TANIA: Of course.

FRANK: Like Ginny… dreaming of a garden wedding for our
shy Scott… who I think is homosexual.

TANIA: Oh.

FRANK: Gay-

TANIA: –Yup –

FRANK: I accept it. But Ginny doesn't want to see it. I wish he
would come out and just tell us.

TANIA: It's hard to open up to parents sometimes. So many
expectations. Give him time. Oh!

*TANIA feels a kick in her belly. She brings FRANK's hand to touch
it. He is moved.*

FRANK: Incredible. We so want grandkids. If we had one,
I think Ginny might consider retiring.

TANIA: Gay couples have kids all the time now.

FRANK: I hope he finds someone. We don't want him to be
alone.

TANIA: Scott is lucky. Pablo got disowned for marrying me.

FRANK: That's shocking

TANIA: His father, who is a very wealthy man in Chile, calls me the "peasant!"

FRANK: You practically have a PhD!!!

TANIA: Because of me, Pablo went from being an insanely rich kid with his own chauffeur, to having to deliver pizzas to try to pay for his last semester of college.

FRANK: All for love. We would be so thrilled if Scott brought home a lovely señorita… or señorito like you.

TANIA: Thank you. Frank… Pablo wants to throw a big garden party this Saturday for his firm –

FRANK: Oh! A party for the firm. Here? That's ambitious.

PABLO enters ready for work, cellphone and very nice briefcase or elegant leather folder in hand.

TANIA: Pablo! There you are.

PABLO: Frank, how are you? Can we talk for a moment? Is Virginia up?

FRANK: She's at a chapter meeting for some fraternity of Women Engineers… but whatever it is, you can tell me.

TANIA: Well, in costing out the price of the fence… we went back to the plans… and well… Oh how do I say this… um …?

PABLO: Frank, did you know that our property line is wider than this?

FRANK: Excuse me?

TANIA: What Pablo means is that… apparently, our property line might be… may be …

PABLO: 2 feet wider.

TANIA: Than we thought.

PABLO: That's what the surveyor confirmed with Tania.

FRANK: He did?

TANIA: Yes. Do you have the papers?

PABLO pulls out the plat from the file folder and hands it to FRANK.

PABLO: Yes. See Frank… it makes sense… see the line.

FRANK: I see it.

PABLO: That's where our property actually ends.

FRANK: Not here?

PABLO: Not here with the fence.

TANIA: That's why your yard looks bigger.

PABLO: Because it's actually bigger. It's backed up by the plat and the surveyors report.

FRANK: *(Beat.)* Oh. What does that mean?

PABLO: It means that these flowerbeds …

TANIA: Your flowerbeds-

PABLO: –are actually on our land.

FRANK: *(Beat.)* I don't think so.

TANIA: I know. I couldn't believe it at first.

FRANK: So that's what those flags in my flowerbed are?

PABLO: Those mark the property line of our property. See how it lines up there and then… Further and further?

FRANK: That silly fence has been up for years. And there's never been a problem before.

248

TANIA: We don't mean to make problems. This doesn't have to be a problem.

PABLO: We just wanted to point out that this stretch actually,

TANIA: Ironically.

PABLO: Belongs to us.

Pause.

FRANK: Oh. Oh my.

PABLO: And since we are about to invest into building this new fence… and for re-sale purposes and what not… we thought it would be best for everyone… if we could line up our fence with the correct property line as soon as possible.

FRANK: I'm so sorry. I'm surprised. And deeply embarrassed.

TANIA: Oh Frank, don't be embarrassed.

PABLO: We were surprised too.

FRANK: I'm flabbergasted. This is terrible. How could this be?

TANIA: Please don't be hard on yourself. We know you didn't do this on purpose!

FRANK: *(Beat.)* On purpose? *(Beat.)* Why would you say such a thing? You think that I… I… that I would stoop so low as to??? You can't just come here and accuse me of things.

TANIA: No one is accusing anyone of anything!

FRANK: I did not put up that fence.

PABLO: Someone did.

FRANK: That is not my business.

PABLO: Actually, it is your business since it affects your property. Had you NO idea it was in the wrong place?

FRANK: No.

PABLO: Really?

FRANK: Am I on trial?

TANIA: No, of course not.

FRANK: Because I feel I am the victim, here. You come and tell me I have to give you something I have thought of as mine... and then treat me like this?

TANIA: I'm sorry. I know this is very awkward. I know how much your garden means to you. I've been loath to bring it up.

FRANK: But you did.

PABLO: We brought it up because something you think is yours is actually... ours. And we need to be adults about this and resolve it.

FRANK: *(Pause.)* I don't know what to say.

PABLO: I know everybody is very sorry and uncomfortable about this. But the fact remains, if we are going to build a fence, it needs to outline the physical line of our actual property.

FRANK: I've worked so hard; the judges come this Sunday.

PABLO: I'm sorry. But the law clearly-

FRANK: STOP! BE QUIET! DO NOT SAY ANOTHER WORD!

PABLO: I didn't... mean to –

FRANK: WHAT DID I SAY, SON? We will talk later.
Excuse me.

Flustered, FRANK runs back to his house.

TANIA: Frank, be careful!

PABLO and TANIA are alone.

TANIA: I can't believe how you handled that!

PABLO: Me? Did you hear him? He's not my father. He told
me to shut up.

TANIA: He said be quiet. And I would too! This is not a
courtroom. They are our friendly neighbors.

PABLO: That's why I also wanted to be very, very clear.

TANIA: Oh you were clearly a jerk! You were also
disrespectful.

PABLO: What?

TANIA: He is our elder. That garden means a lot to him.

PABLO: I know. But take it from me, when things are sensitive
is exactly when clarity and reason need to prevail.

TANIA: But is it worth it? I mean, we bought the place
assuming that our yard ended here and their flowerbed
was theirs! We were grateful for that.

PABLO: But this is good news for us!

TANIA: This does not feel like good news.

PABLO: So what do you want to do?

TANIA: Forget what the contract says. Keep everything like
this. Let's not be greedy! And be happy with that. We go
and apologize to them and move on.

PABLO: Apologize? For pointing out they are stealing from us?

TANIA: Pablo, get out of your shark mentality. These are our neighbors.

PABLO: Fine!

TANIA: Fine! Good. So we go and apologize.

PABLO: And thank them for taking $38,000 out of our pocket.

TANIA: What are you talking about?

PABLO: That stretch is 80 square feet. Which in this neighborhood is $478 per square foot which is the equivalent of $38,200. Today. And who knows how much more it will be worth in the future. You feel we can just give that away?

TANIA: That much? That's more than twice what my Dad used to make.

PABLO: You want to forfeit part of the land that rightfully belongs to us? Give some old people we barely know something for nothing? And pay extra property taxes to boot?

TANIA: That doesn't feel right either.

PABLO: I know this is emotional, but we have to be smart about this.

TANIA: And kind… we have to be kind. It can't be just about the money.

PABLO: Listen, they are upset. It's natural. But they will just have to get over it. This competition comes every year. The wood fence we are buying will help us both in the long run. We need to carry on and right this wrong. They will adjust.

TANIA: How can you be sure?

PABLO: They are good and decent people, aren't they?

VIGNETTE 5 - WEDNESDAY

PABLO exits. TANIA greets the crowd of Gomez Landscape Technicians as they enter. They discuss the work that needs to be done. Then she exits. Maybe the workers have brought a boom box, playing music. Maybe they throw bags of dirt to each other. The technicians get to work, swapping the flags for twenty-four inch stakes, clearing the garbage and junk and pulling out the wilted hydrangeas in TANIA's yard. Once all of this is finished, the landscape technicians exit. Lights shift.

SCENE 5 - WEDNESDAY NIGHT

FRANK and VIRGINIA enter their yard. It's late. They have a flashlight. There are now four thirty inch stakes instead of flags.

VIRGINIA: Frank, you need to calm down.

FRANK: I am calm. I'm just upset.

VIRGINIA: This is silly. They might see us.

FRANK: They are asleep. And I want to see the damage. I want you to see it. They seemed so kind and so civilized.

Gasps when he lights TANIA's wilted Hydrangea's and see they are gone.

But who rips out hydrangeas? They could have been saved. Those poor plants are being murdered!

VIRGINIA: It's not good for you to get so worked up about it.

FRANK: These are living things that were planted with purpose and care. Now look at this. It used to be flags... now it's –

253

VIRGINIA: Stakes! Why are they out so far?

FRANK: Ginny! That's where the new fence is going to go. They say their property is two feet further than the old fence.

VIRGINIA: What? This far? That's crazy. When did they tell you?

FRANK: While I was clipping the ivy. As a favor to them. I'm taking a picture.

VIRGINIA: They want to take our land?

FRANK: The dandy Esquire nonchalantly told me that they own this much of our property.

VIRGINIA: Where did they get that idea?

FRANK: From the documents attached to their mortgage. And then the survey they did… showed the same thing. They have documents. Do we?

VIRGINIA: It's been decades. God know where ours are.

FRANK: Did you ever think we were taking land that wasn't ours?

VIRGINIA: Us? Of course not! What did you say?

FRANK: I told him to "Hold his tongue and shut his BIG mouth" and I shook my fist and told him I'd see him in court.

VIRGINIA: Really? You did? To a lawyer?

FRANK: Basically! And then I walked away.

VIRGINIA: You walked away? Please don't tell me you rolled over like a circus dog.

FRANK: No– I was vicious. And intimidating.

VIRGINIA: You cannot cede an inch with this. You hear? An inch becomes a foot becomes a yard.

FRANK: I assure you. Walking away wasn't a retreat.

VIRGINIA: Chamberlain looked the other way when it came to Poland. Nothing appeases greed.

FRANK: I've been documenting the destruction all evening.

VIRGINIA: But we need more than photos. We need to find those documents. This is our property!

FRANK: We were so nice to them. And they seemed to like us. What have we done to deserve this?

VIRGINIA: Nothing but bring them wine and dark chocolate.

FRANK: Exactly. You know how I worked on the flowerbeds. Just to have a fence slam into them. Sever them. Days before the garden judgment. I'll never win Best Garden. Thanks to them, I may not even be in the running ever. Phillip Saxon will gloat all year.

VIRGINIA: Frank, don't get all lathered up about this. Tomorrow we'll give those ambitious kids a gentle lesson in maturity. I'll do the talking. OK? You get too upset.

FRANK: Fine.

VIRGINIA: Believe me, I will put a stop to this whole travesty.

VIGNETTE 6 - THURSDAY

The Gomez Gardeners arrive again with wood panels and posts to make the fence while TANIA rakes. They set the poles and lean the wood panels up against the house. They tidy up the yard as TANIA rakes onstage. FRANK looks from the window upstairs. Then FRANK and VIRGINIA enter.

SCENE 6 - THURSDAY

Out in TANIA and PABLO's Yard. She is raking.

VIRGINIA: Good morning. Tania.

TANIA: Good morning, Virginia. Frank.

VIRGINIA: Where's Pablo?

TANIA: Pablo is at work. I so wanted to apologize for what happened yesterday.

VIRGINIA: I should say so.

TANIA: We wanted to all talk together... but then we got ahead of ourselves... and we didn't handle the situation as... adroitly as we should have.

FRANK: Uh-huh.

VIRGINIA: Thank you. I appreciate it.

TANIA: You have been so gracious and kind. We didn't mean for this to get tense.

VIRGINIA: Good. So why don't we all take a big, deep breath. And pause. It would be great if you could give us a chance to find our documents... and study the survey... and let us slowly digest everything. Let Frank go through the competition this Sunday... and then we can revisit the issue.

TANIA: But the fence people are here. I thought you wanted a nice wood fence to help you win? Because I think a fence –

VIRGINIA: I think a fence is... imperative. But Tania, there needs to be a compromise about when, and maybe where.

TANIA: OK. So where do you think we should put the new fence?

FRANK: Right where the old fence is!

TANIA: *(Beat.)* That's not much of a compromise.

VIRGINIA: A temporary compromise… until we come up with a better one. When all the facts are in.

TANIA: But I think all the facts are in.

VIRGINIA: We need more time. Please.

TANIA: I don't have it! We have a lot of other pressures and we need this fence in the right place as soon as possible. Frank can use all year to re-plan his garden for next year. I'm sorry.

VIRGINIA: That is so… unkind.

FRANK: It's the pesticides, isn't it? They get a bad reputation. But I need them. I'm telling you: Organic gardens get eaten alive.

TANIA: I know! That's the point of organic gardens!!!!

Beat.

I realize no one wants to be in this situation.

FRANK: Then don't be in this situation.

VIRGINIA: All we are asking for is a little more time …

TANIA: And we don't have that. We have this barbeque to throw on Saturday.

FRANK: Oh.

VIRGINIA: A barbeque?

TANIA: It's a very important line-in-the-sand barbeque.

VIRGINIA: You're telling me you are going to destroy Frank's flowers, his vision, and art, for a hamburger party!

257

TANIA: It's "BBQ Jacks" and it's catered. This party is much more complicated than that …

VIRGINIA: This can't be happening.

TANIA: It's for Pablo's law firm.

VIRGINIA: Oh no.

TANIA: You understand… he has something to prove. We need this party. I know… this is very upsetting. But it seems that for years, for one reason or another, you have ended up taking –

VIRGINIA: –We have taken nothing. –

TANIA: –Obtaining part of the Whitefield lawn which belongs to us.

FRANK: Obtaining?

TANIA: I'm sorry, but we can't let you… borrow… this land anymore. We need it.

FRANK: And what are you going to do? Butcher it? Ruin my chances this year with the garden competition.

TANIA: Frank, you've had many years to try to win with that garden.

FRANK reacts.

I only have this one chance to help my husband impress his partners. And the sooner we get this done. The sooner we can all get on with the healing process

VIRGINIA: Healing process. What kind of mumbo jumbo is that?

TANIA: It's the process you go through when things don't go your way.

VIRGINIA: Things will go our way.

TANIA: Maybe not this time. My husband says the law is on our side.

FRANK: Well, possession is nine tenths of the law!

TANIA: Really? Then every thief would use that as an argument.

FRANK: Did you just call us thieves?

TANIA: NO! NO. Not at all. I was just poking holes in your argument.

VIRGINIA: You are poking holes in Frank's heart.

TANIA: I feel caught in the middle. And I feel you are ganging up on me. Pablo feels strongly –

FRANK: It's barbaric!

TANIA: Barbaric? You think reclaiming what is ours… is barbaric?

FRANK starts to pull the stakes out and throw them into TANIA's yard.

VIRGINIA: Listen Missy, I'm not sure that it is yours.

TANIA: Frank, what are you doing

FRANK throws another stake over.

You can have a surveyor come out. He'll just tell you what he told us.

VIRGINIA: If you gave us some time, but that seems impossible!

TANIA: I'm sorry… it is pandemonium. We have people here right now to help make this into something presentable.

In a matter of two days it will all be over. And it will look good. And we can move on.

FRANK: We have had you in our home. I thought we were going to be friends.

TANIA: I want to be friends.

FRANK: Like this?

FRANK runs off, upset.

TANIA: I'm so sorry, Frank.

VIRGINIA: *(To TANIA.)* You are stressing him out!

TANIA: Virginia, I don't want to upset him… but I assure you, this fence… will make us better neighbors in the long run. Not –

VIRGINIA: You can't just move in and take over. I won't let you bully us with your native plants, and workers, and "BBQ Jacks"! You! Stop!

TANIA: You aren't their boss. I am.

VIRGINIA: STOP You. Stop! Put that down! Don't look like that at me. STOP! Do you understand English???? How do I say STOP in Spanish?

TANIA: You say "Alto! Soy una pinche vieja"

Landscape technicians all react.

VIRGINIA: What did you say?

TANIA: Nothing. Oh God.

VIRGINIA: Peter, Paul and Mary! I could be your mother!

TANIA: I should not use language like that.

VIRGINIA: I may not understand what you said but I hootin' well know what you meant.

TANIA: But you weren't being kind either. You pushed all my buttons.

VIRGINIA: I've got your number, missy. Don't mess with Virginia –– Butley.

VIRGINIA walks off. TANIA bursts into tears..

VIGNETTE 7 - THURSDAY EVENING

The Gomez Landscape Technicians begin to pull out the wire fence as FRANK enters. He crosses to the fence and throws a fit. He takes his clippers and gardening caddy and exits into his house. The Landscape Technicians place the fence up against the house and exit. VIRGINIA comes outside holding a coffee cup and smoking, surveying the damage, aka progress. She blows smoke into the Del Valle yard. It's clear that she's not a chain smoker, but that she smokes when she is stressed. FRANK comes out and joins her.

SCENE 7 - THURSDAY EVENING

FRANK: She insulted you?

VIRGINIA: Called me names.

FRANK: Like what?

VIRGINIA: I-DON'T-KNOW. . Horrible words in Spanish that all her workers understood. Very humiliating.

Beat.

So I talked to an attorney.

FRANK: And what did he say?

VIRGINIA: She said that we don't have much recourse. That legally, it appears that they own our land… and they have the right to claim it.

FRANK: Surely that can't be all we can do. We didn't knowingly steal the land. We would never do such a thing.

VIRGINIA: I know. I know.

FRANK: We didn't even put the fence up. That was the stupid Whitefield stepson that made that mistake. I never noticed our yard was bigger!

VIRGINIA: Frank, these are not our sins. There's no need for us to notice because we did nothing. We are innocent victims.

FRANK: God, I miss smoking.

VIRGINIA: Now everything we love is bad.

FRANK: Like margarine, and white rice, and... Cat Stevens.

VIRGINIA: Shenanigans. Why does everything have to become so complicated?

FRANK: All we did was take something ugly and make it beautiful.

VIRGINIA: And now we are being treated like criminals.

FRANK: They must be Democrats, don't you think?

VIRGINIA: With that level of sanctimony– of course they're Democrats.

FRANK: And for $250 an hour, the attorney said there was nothing he could do?

VIRGINIA: Well, she did bring up one thing.

FRANK: What was that?

VIRGINIA: Well, we've worked the flower garden in a purposeful and public way for many years.

FRANK: Yes.

VIRGINIA: And she says there are certain provisions that "allow ownership for someone that has lived on and tended neglected land."

FRANK: Is she talking about invoking squatters rights????

VIRGINIA: Oddly enough, it might be a legal recourse.

FRANK: Squatters rights?

VIRGINIA: Adverse possession is the legal term.

FRANK: Are you insane?

VIRGINIA: I'm just relaying the information, Frank.

FRANK: What would the Potomac Horticultural Society say about that? How could we look people in the eye! Can you just imagine Phillip Saxon's reaction? What would we say to him?

VIRGINIA: We would look Phillip Saxon in the eye *(Looks.)* and say: "Listen buddy, we're between a squat and hard place."

FRANK: No! Good God... that is a horrible idea. Squatters are poor people that are desperate.

VIRGINIA: Not always.

FRANK: Is there an uglier word in the English language than SQUAT? I mean, squat is what you do when you defecate. Squat is what peasant women do in the fields to have babies. Squat is what degenerate bums do to get out of buying land. You tell that lady, that lawyer, that we cannot be squatters.

VIRGINIA: Jiminy Crickets! Then say goodbye to your perfectly symmetrical garden that you have worked on for a decade.

FRANK: Why are you yelling at me?

VIRGINIA: Just because you don't like what you hear doesn't mean you shouldn't listen! Squatter's rights are also about justice. Those laws exist to protect hard working people from greedy and neglectful landowners. And God knows, you have worked hard.

FRANK: I have.

VIRGINIA: We worked the land in good faith, with good intentions, with the full belief that this here soil was ours.

FRANK: We certainly did.

VIRGINIA: Only to have something we love and cherish be ripped away from us, by the roots, bringing down the value and aesthetic of our entire home.

FRANK: Selfish kids.

VIRGINIA: They are fully formed adults with growing earning potential who will stop at nothing. We are simply a couple of old people on the brink of retirement who are in their way. And they will mow us down for our lawn.

FRANK: Millennials. I don't think we should let them get away with this.

VIRGINIA: Now you're talking turkey. Let's show these unscrupulous brats what power to the people really means.

VIGNETTE 8 - THURSDAY EVENING

VIRGINIA grabs the coffee cup with the cigarette. Maybe she throws her cigarette butt in the DEL VALLE yard and exits. FRANK remains on the bench. Time passes.

SCENE 8 - THURSDAY EVENING

Night time. FRANK is outside. PABLO enters with a beer.

PABLO: I know it's after midnight, but do you mind if I join you?

FRANK: Yes, I do.

PABLO grabs a folded chair, has some difficulty unfolding it, and sits, facing FRANK.

FRANK: Did you just get home from work?

PABLO: Yes. My wife is horribly upset about the… incident this morning.

FRANK: Women get so emotional when they are pregnant.

PABLO: I hear Virginia is not too happy either.

Beat.

I also assume she's not pregnant.

Beat. Men size each other up.

FRANK: No one is happy.

PABLO: You tried to make my wife feel small.

FRANK: Maybe she feels small, because she called my wife names.

PABLO: Virginia threatened Tania.

FRANK: Pablo. You are creating havoc over twenty-three inches.

PABLO: It's eighty square feet, at least. If it's so valuable to you, I'll sell it to you at market price.

FRANK: Ah, so it's all about the money.

PABLO: No. But it is a way to come to terms. A rational way to make peace.

FRANK: I shouldn't have to spend that kind of cash. I've been tending this garden for years. Its value comes from my care.

PABLO: Maybe you should be grateful you've had it for free for so long.

FRANK: Ginny and I have been researching adverse possession.

PABLO: You are invoking squatter's rights?

FRANK: I'm thinking we might have a case.

PABLO: Frank, I like you. I really do. And let me tell you, you don't want to get in a legal argument with Smith, Krause, and Wilson.

FRANK: Sometimes the little man wins.

PABLO: You've never been the little man, Frank Butley. And we can't have another argument like we did this morning.

FRANK: That was no argument. It was an incident.

PABLO: I have sixty colleagues coming on Saturday. We have every right to do what we are doing.

FRANK: But what about my garden and the years of toil, sweat and love I've poured into it? You are sacrificing all the work I have done. For what: to make it look ordinary and common? Just days after you said you loved it. Are you a liar, Pablo?

PABLO: *(Confessing in a hushed tone.)* I do like your garden. I like its grace and elegance.

Loudly for TANIA's benefit in case she's listening from inside.

BUT Tania's garden is BETTER, because it is… *(Sigh.)* NATURAL.

FRANK: Nature is not why people move to this neighborhood. You could have bought a house with a chicken coop in in hippy dippy Takoma Park and been as messy and native gardeny as you wanted. But you didn't want that, did you? You wanted to put down roots here… in a stately neighborhood with all the other K-Street lawyers and doctors and lobbyists. Why did you move here if you want to change everything?

PABLO: We don't want to change everything. We just want to add our touch to the landscape. Tania believes your plants are eroding the ecosystem. They are foreign to the natural environment.

FRANK: So Tania has a problem with my plants because they are from somewhere else? -Because they are…immigrant plants?

PABLO: *(Beat.)* No. Tania's problem is that your plants are … colonialists with gross disregard for the indigenous population.

FRANK: I'm surprised that you of all people, Pablo, would defend this type of… botanical xenophobia.

PABLO: Back away Frank.

FRANK: No. You tell Tania to back away from my defenseless plants. This is a border dispute. And I'm not giving up one inch of my yard without a fight.

PABLO: You don't want to fight with me, Frank.

FRANK: I would say the same, Pablo. I've been in this town a long time. I spent thirty-seven years at the Agency.

PABLO: The Agency?

FRANK: The Agency. I know P-owerful P-eople, PA--blo.

FRANK exits. PABLO pours his beer on FRANK's flower bed and exits..

VIGNETTE NINE - FRIDAY MORNING

TANIA enters with a tray of lemonade and a pint of ice cream with spoon for herself and greets the Gomez Garden Landscape Technicians as they come in, delivering flats of flowers, a shovel and a post hole digger. One sits on one of FRANK's chairs to finish the lemonade. Then they exit.

SCENE 9 - FRIDAY MORNING

TANIA: Maybe we should just cancel the party– stand down before we fall down.

PABLO: What? The plants and fence go in today. My entire firm arrives tomorrow afternoon.

TANIA: But Pablo, I was terrible. I called Virginia names!

PABLO: I'm sure she deserved it! Don't go soft, Tania. This is not about flowers. It's about principles. This is war.

TANIA: It's not war. Not yet. I need to go talk to her. I'll make her understand our point of view. The pressure we are under.

PABLO: I don't think you should. In fact I say no!

TANIA: No?!!!!

PABLO: *(Oh-Oh- backtracks.)* Frank threatened me.

TANIA: Sweet Frank? No way.

PABLO: Oh. He showed some big "cojones" last night.

TANIA: That term is ridiculous. Testicles are the most delicate part of a man. What did you say?

PABLO: Nothing! All I know is he said we are wild, messy people and we should go native somewhere else.

TANIA: He did not say that!

PABLO: And he says he knows powerful people. He says he works for the "agency".

TANIA: What does that mean?

PABLO: In Chile it means very bad things.

TANIA: Do you think Frank Butley is CIA?

PABLO: No! I googled him. He's GSA. As in General Services. His agency manages other agencies. They buy phones and soap and toilet paper. *(Convincing himself.)* Not scary.

TANIA: But you said he knows powerful people. And she's a defense contractor. What have we gotten ourselves in to?

PABLO: Nobody tells me what I can do or not do. Not in my house. NOT IN MY BACK YARD!

TANIA: Pablo, are you feeling OK?

PABLO: It's nothing. He's getting to me. But we will not be bullied and threatened into submission.

TANIA: Pablo, they are our neighbors. We have to live next to them. Our children will have to live next to them.

PABLO: They are researching adverse possession.

TANIA: Virginia and Frank Butley are invoking squatter rights? Do they have a case?

PABLO: I told them they didn't.

TANIA: But do they?

PABLO: They need to have been openly and notoriously using a piece of land as would an owner for a certain number of years.

TANIA: They have. Haven't they?

PABLO: My father lost a lot of land in Chile due to squatters. It was so demoralizing for him. I will not let that happen to me. Not in this way. It's ridiculous.

TANIA: I thought squatter rights were for poor people.

PABLO: It's a travesty of justice.

TANIA: But you say they don't have a case?

PABLO: No, I didn't say that. I told them they didn't want to fight Smith, Krause and Wilson.

TANIA: You told them to not fight the Man?

PABLO: Yes.

TANIA: Because we are now: the Man?

PABLO: Yes.

TANIA: One thing is this being between two neighbors. But now you set up that small old couple against a huge industrial law firm... and everything seems very different.

PABLO: Isn't that what the struggle is for you? Moving up? Buying a house? Becoming the boss? Isn't this the American Dream?

TANIA: Enabling large institutions to crush little old white people? No!

PABLO: They are Republicans!

TANIA: They are still people!

PABLO: Tania you know better than anyone that we don't reverse years of discrimination, of growing up like second-class citizens, of being the "minority" because in one instance we have the upper hand.

TANIA: We? Wait a second, Señor Mister. You weren't called a spic in second grade or asked if you were illegal when you applied for a waitressing job. You had maids and butlers, and took cello lessons, and vacationed in Europe. You grew up with the biggest silver spoon in your mouth of anyone I know. You were never treated as inferior in Chile in anyway.

PABLO: No. But I became a minority the moment I moved to this country. And I know that we have to WANT to be the MAN or nothing will ever change.

TANIA: No! It's all this Man, Machista, Cojones talk that is the problem. I'm going to talk to Virginia, woman-to-woman. And get this resolved.

TANIA marches inside, PABLO dumps a bunch of acorns and dead leaves on the Butley yard.

VIGNETTE 10 - FRIDAY MORNING

Morning. VIRGINIA enters with a cup of coffee and a newspaper. She surveys the damage. She crosses in to the Del Valle yard and dumps her coffee in their birdbath or/and VIRGINIA might get bit by a mosquito and go further and spray the Del Valle lawn with a little pesticide. She then goes to her deck, opens her Washington Post and sits, aggressively, in wait. TANIA comes out, spots her… and approaches.

271

SCENE 10 - FRIDAY MORNING

TANIA: Virginia. I don't mean to intrude on your morning.

VIRGINIA: Tania. I've taken the day off. Don't you have a big fancy schmanzy party happening tomorrow?

TANIA: Pablo and I are good people. We don't want to hurt you.

VIRGINIA: Frank and I are good people too.

TANIA: I'm so sorry I said those things to you.

VIRGINIA: Thank you. Well, it wasn't my finest moment either. And at least I learned something. Swearing in Spanish seems so much more satisfying.

TANIA: I promise, you won't hear that type of language again.

VIRGINIA: Would you like a seat? You must be tired.

TANIA: Thank you.

VIRGINIA: You should take a load off. Here let me help you prop up your feet. Your poor ankles.

TANIA: I never thought I would swell up like this.

VIRGINIA: None of us do. And then it happens. But it's so worth it. You'll see. Kids add a lot of color to your life. I love being a mother.

TANIA: Virginia –

VIRGINIA: Call me Ginny.

TANIA: Ginny, you need to know, I never intended for this to get like this.

VIRGINIA: I know. I know. The men got involved and suddenly …

TANIA: Exactly! The men talked and then things just blew up. And I don't want this to get worse. I knew if I came here, and we talked that would be a step in the right direction. There has to be a compromise.

VIRGINIA: I am so relieved to hear you say that.

TANIA: It's just been so overwhelming and all at once. The pregnancy, the move, and the firm and now all this stuff. The entire office is coming tomorrow. The baby is due in five weeks …

VIRGINIA: The only thing that matters is you need to take care of yourself. Keeping you and the baby healthy has to be your priority.

TANIA: Yes. Of course.

VIRGINIA: So ironic this all had to happen the same week as Frank's gardening competition.

TANIA: I'm so sorry about the timing.

VIRGINIA: Well I know throwing this party isn't easy either.

TANIA: What we do for our men.

VIRGINIA: Our crazy, neurotic men.

TANIA: Impulsive, and more impulsive.

VIRGINIA: Wanting to win, wanting it all.

TANIA: Ah– BOYS!

They laugh.

VIRGINIA: Although, we women want to win too. Don't we?

TANIA: Yes but for different reasons.

VIRGINIA: Very different.

TANIA: Pablo and I are just trying to build a better future for our family.

VIRGINIA: Yes, of course you are. It's the…United Statesean dream.

They laugh.

VIRGINIA: I think I might have a very similar story to yours. I grew up with very few things. Not in New Mexico. But Buffalo. Like you, I made my way into the world. I started earning money… oh my… the flushness of it, the possibility of it, gave me quite a rush. Made me want things even more. But things that I could not buy. Like respect.

TANIA: Ginny, we didn't mean to be disrespectful.

VIRGINIA: Of course not. But you were.

TANIA: You do understand we do have the right to build the fence.

VIRGINIA: Yes, I do. But think about it. Your husband makes an impulsive decision that in six days destroys decades of someone else's hard work. Don't you find that kind of… entitled?

TANIA: But you are the ones that felt entitled to plant flowers wherever you want …

VIRGINIA: Can you hear yourself? You are accusing us of what? Planting flowers. Now what kind of crime is that?

TANIA: It's our land. And those flowers are detrimental to the environment.

VIRGINIA: Great! Save the world, but screw your neighbors. What kind of environment is that? You said you didn't understand how this all spiraled. I'm an engineer… So I'm explaining it to you: Your desire for more started this all.

TANIA: You mean my greed?

VIRGINIA: I didn't say that word. Did I?

TANIA: No one has ever called me greedy before.

VIRGINIA: You are a woman. They probably masked it with
more generous words… like ambitious and determined …
or bitchy. It's so unfair. Believe me, I know.

TANIA: I'm greedy for hoping to get what I paid for? So
Virginia, what are you? How did you get more land than
you bought?

VIRGINIA: As far as I remember, this has been like this for a
very long time.

TANIA: And that's the crux of it. You have because you have.
Because you are used to it. Stolen goods are not stolen,
they are acquired. The world is already so entrenched
in your favor you don't even need to recognize how you
benefit from inequity. You are blind to your privilege! And
you don't stop unless you are held accountable. You…
You people… you…

VIRGINIA: You? What do you mean… by: You people?

TANIA: *(Beat.)* You and Frank.

VIRGINIA: You mean senior people?

TANIA: I mean… you and Frank.

VIRGINIA: Do you mean white people?

TANIA: Do not put words in my mouth.

VIRGINIA: You are attacking us because we are rich and
white. That's classism and racism. Would you make this
kind of ruckus if Frank and I had been black? Or Latino?
Would you attack us if we had a cactus in our back yard?

TANIA: Oh, because Mexicans only want cacti in their back yard?

VIRGINIA: See! You <u>are</u> Mexican.

TANIA: I am Mexican! And American! And Latinx!

VIRGINIA: Latin– what?

TANIA: X!

VIRGINIA: Why are you yelling?

TANIA: I want to make sure you hear me, even if you don't want to!

VIRGINIA: Ah-ha! See? There it is, the big chip on the shoulder. You would handle this different if we were different.

TANIA: No. I would not. If you were my Latinx neighbor and you had two feet of our yard, you better believe I would still come and claim it. But… I bet you would be a lot less resistant to our rightful legal rights if we "fit in better."

VIRGINIA: I know you mock us. You think you're better than us because you're young and hip. That, young lady, is ageism.

TANIA: Virginia, the only "ism" you feel is your own narcissism. How you managed to paint yourself as the victim in all of this is a feat of self-delusion. We are the ones that have been cheated. Not you.

VIRGINIA: We are upright, taxpaying, law-abiding citizens.

TANIA: So are we.

VIRGINIA: But you are taking things we love away from us.

TANIA: You know, I came over to apologize. …

VIRGINIA: And I graciously accept your apology.

TANIA: I don't think I am giving it to you anymore.

VIRGINIA: Honey, you are pregnant. It's making you
irrational.

TANIA: I'm passionately rational!

TANIA turns to go, then stops.

I've never been entitled a day in my life. Except now.
When the title of our land actually says we are entitled
to the land we bought and that you have. You are the
occupation. But we shall overcome. You will not stop us.

VIGNETTE 11 - FRIDAY MORNING

*Maybe or maybe not the workers arrive as a fight between TANIA and
VIRGINIA comes to a head. But the INSPECTOR definitely enters and
looks at her clipboard. S/he slaps a stop order on to the tree and exits.
TANIA freaks out and runs in to the house to call PABLO. VIRGINIA
stand tall.*

SCENE 11 - FRIDAY AFTERNOON/EVENING

Split scene. FRANK and VIRGINIA's house.

VIRGINIA: She called us racist!

FRANK: She actually said those words?

VIRGINIA: Not exactly but it was implied.

FRANK: Did you tell her that I considered voting for Obama?

VIRGINIA: No. I wouldn't dignify her with that.

TANIA and PABLO's house.

PABLO: I hurried home the moment you called me.

TANIA: And then the officials. They came. They came.

PABLO: Where are all the fence workers?

TANIA: Pablo, a stop order from the DC government is a STOP ORDER. I had to send them home.

PABLO AND FRANK: Sons of bitches.

FRANK: Just because we disagree does not mean we are racist. How could she think us racist?

VIRGINIA: Who knows with these people.

PABLO: Frank said he knew people.

TANIA: They came, with their little tablet and little pen and looked over everything and then they slapped a big yellow sign on my tree.

VIRGINIA AND TANIA: It's code.

VIRGINIA: Why do they always have to turn it into a race thing?

FRANK: Every time.

VIRGINIA: I think it gives them a sort of moral impunity… permission to do what they want. But the stop order gave them a scare.

FRANK: Wait. A stop order?

VIRGINIA: Yes. I called in some favors and the DC inspector came out right away. And sure enough, they found some "gross irregularities" and issued a stop order and a fine!

FRANK: No!

VIRGINIA: I thought you would be happy.

FRANK: Happy! No. Have you looked at their yard? We need that fence to keep the mess at bay! The judges will look at this and I'll be the laughing stock!

PABLO: How did we break code?

TANIA: Our fence is six feet and one inch. It should only be six feet. We are on the wrong inch of the law!

PABLO: But it's not even up! It's not even a fence yet.

TANIA: Apparently, the inspector established that wood had "specific intent" of becoming a fence.

PABLO: God, I hate the law.

TANIA: How they got the DC inspector here so fast is beyond me.

PABLO: GSA!

TANIA: Such a home field advantage. They were just looking for a reason to stop us. And they did. So there is a stop order. And a huge $2,000 fine.

VIRGINIA: I'm at my wits end. We are decent people. Did we not welcome them with open arms?

FRANK: We brought them wine and chocolate.

VIRGINIA: We bought them FINE wine and chocolate… so they would know… how extra happy we were to have them here.

FRANK: And this is how they repay us.

VIRGINIA AND PABLO: Bastards!

TANIA: The barbeque is tomorrow.

PABLO: I'm going to have to cancel. I'm going to have to go back and tell everyone that it's off.

TANIA: Pablo. You can't.

PABLO: The only thing that looks good in our lawn is Frank's friggin' flower bed… we are doomed.

TANIA: Don't talk like that, Pablo.

PABLO: I have to look reality in the eye. There will never be Smith, Krause, Wilson, and Del Valle.

TANIA: Shut up, Pablo. And stop talking nonsense.

PABLO: I'll never make partner.

FRANK: I'll never take Best Garden.

PABLO AND FRANK: We've lost.

VIRGINIA AND TANIA: No!

FRANK: I'm withdrawing from the competition.

VIRGINIA: No. Let the judges see what we are up against. It will build good will.

TANIA: We just haven't had a chance to win… but we will. We will.

PABLO: It's Friday afternoon. A stop order is a bureaucratic nightmare… of waiting for the judge, paying a fine. There's no way any contractor can legally get that fence up by tomorrow.

VIRGINIA: Frank, those plants are living things and you are their only line of defense.

FRANK: I can't bear to think of it.

TANIA: Pablo, where is the man who was sixth in his class? Where is the man who stood up to his father and demanded to marry the woman he loves? You are telling me that Frank and Virginia are bigger and stronger than you?

VIRGINIA: Are you telling me that after all that de-grubbing, all that pesticide, all that Miracle Grow… you've decided to sit back and watch your beloved flowers be trampled by a wood fence?

PABLO AND FRANK: Hell no. You're right.

VIRGINIA AND TANIA: Justice is on our side.

TANIA: So we have a stop order. Time for you to start writing and documenting a defense.

PABLO: No. Let me see your hands.

TANIA: My puffy pregnant hands?

PABLO: These are the hands of people who scrubbed floors, and worked the land. It's time for me to buck up.

VIRGINIA: I thought she was coming over to apologize. And instead she taunted us.

FRANK: Enough. They must be stopped!

PABLO: I'm not a contractor. I'm just a man… on my property, tilling my own land.

TANIA: Surely, that's not a crime. Even in DC.

VIRGINIA: They treat us like criminals.

PABLO: Time for my delicate Chilean hands to get rough.

VIRGINIA: Frank, let's get tough.

FRANK: Tough is my middle name.

TANIA: Let's build our own fence… between us… and the imperialist gardens beyond.

FRANK AND PABLO AND TANIA AND VIRGINIA: We will not stand down.

VIGNETTE 12 - FRIDAY EVENING

PABLO tears the Stop Order into pieces and confettis the yards with it

TANIA and PABLO exit in to their house. VIRGINIA grabs the chair off the deck and moves it to between the flowerbeds. FRANK enters with a chain. He crosses to VIRGINIA. They chain her to the chair. FRANK then picks up a shovel and begins to patrol the property line. TANIA and PABLO come out.

SCENE 12 - FRIDAY EVENING

VIRGINIA and FRANK are chanting, "Give our plants a chance!" as the scene begins.

PABLO: What are you doing?

FRANK: Border patrol.

TANIA: You are on my property, Mr. Butley.

FRANK: I'm protecting my property, Señorita Del Valle.

TANIA: That's almost Doctor Del Valle to you, Butley.

PABLO: Frank, I'm going to have ask you to move aside.

FRANK: To build a fence. Never.

TANIA: Virginia, please get up.

VIRGINIA: No can do.

PABLO: Don't tell me you are doing a sit in.

VIRGINIA: They were effective for young folk back then.
    Maybe they will work for us old folk now.

FRANK: Are you building the fence by yourselves?

PABLO: We are.

VIRGINIA: But there's a stop order.

TANIA: Well, a little sign can't stop us.

PABLO: We are taking back what you took from us.

TANIA crosses upstage to get the post hold digger.

FRANK: Oh no you don't!

FRANK picks up an acorn; he throws it at PABLO. An acorn fight ensues.

PABLO: Desgraciado. Que te creì.

VIRGINIA: GET OFF MY LAWN!

TANIA: It's our lawn.

VIRGINIA: Get off my lawn before I call the police.

TANIA: It's our lawn. Thought we could talk this out. But no. There is no talking with you people.

VIRGINIA: You people. Did you hear that? That's it!

VIRGINIA runs off to call the police.

FRANK: This is my property. My land.

TANIA: No, it's my land. I'm building my fence to keep you out!

PABLO: And you're going to pay for it.

TANIA raises the post hole digger above the flowerbed.

FRANK: You can't! You can't do that.

PABLO: Don't tell my wife what to do.

TANIA plunges the digger into the flowerbed.

FRANK: NOOOOO!

Wait a minute– I planted those flowers. I paid for those seeds and bulbs. I can prove it. You can't keep them on your side.

PABLO: He's right.

She reaches down and plucks one out. She throws it at FRANK.

TANIA: Here you go. I'm returning your flowers to you.

FRANK: No! Stop!

TANIA: You stop, Frank.

FRANK: It's a massacre.

TANIA starts pulling out a lot of flowers. Suddenly VIRGINIA comes out with a chainsaw.

VIRGINIA: Unhand my husband's flowers. Or else!

VIRGINIA revs up the chainsaw and crosses to the tree.

TANIA: No!

VIRGINIA starts to attack the tree.

PABLO: Not the tree!

TANIA: My oak tree.

PABLO: No!

VIRGINIA: This will make us better neighbors, Pablo.

PABLO: Stop!

TANIA: I'm going to call the police.

PABLO: I can't be part of an incident!

TANIA: None of this would have happened if it wasn't for the barbeque.

PABLO: No, they would have been happy with a normal lawn … but no… you had to go exotic.

TANIA: Native is not exotic.

FRANK: It's ugly. It goes against the historical landscaping of this neighborhood.

TANIA: It was here before the neighborhood ever existed.

PABLO: Oh my God.

FRANK makes to squirt TANIA with the hose – PABLO jumps in front of her. Only a fine mist comes out.

PABLO: Demonios!!!

TANIA: Argh!!!!!

PABLO: Tania are you OK?

TANIA: ARGHHH my water …

PABLO: The baby. It's early.

VIRGINIA: The baby!

TANIA: It's coming.

VIRGINIA: Tania, just breathe.

TANIA: I am breathing!

TANIA screams.

VIRGINIA: Your breathing is all wrong. Breathe like this…

PABLO: We have to get to the hospital.

TANIA: I don't think so …

PABLO: I'm getting dizzy.

VIRGINIA: You are hyperventilating Pablo.

VIRGINIA slaps PABLO.

Stay focused.

TANIA: Forget it. I don't think I can walk any more.

PABLO: Wait, you can't have the baby out here in the field! Like …

TANIA: Like a peasant!???!

FRANK: Is she going to squat?

VIRGINIA: Get a grip, Frank.

TANIA screams.

VIRGINIA: *(To TANIA.)* Tania, honey, it's OK, lean on me.

TANIA: Ginny, I'm so scared. Help. My baby …

VIRGINIA: Just breathe, Tania. The baby is going to be fine.

FRANK: Can you take another step?

TANIA: I have to lie down.

PABLO: Not here… in the dirt.

VIRGINIA: It's going to have to be here.

FRANK takes off his sweater.

FRANK: Lie on my sweater.

PABLO: Breathe breathe breathe. I'm so sorry Tania. This got too big… we lost sight.

TANIA: It's OK

Screams.

Ay Dios Mio de los Santos!!!!

PABLO: I love you.

TANIA: Puta Madre!

FRANK: Your Spanish is so much better than you think.

VIRGINIA: Breathe.

FRANK: Breathe.

PABLO: Breathe. Honey.

VIRGINIA: We are here. It's going to be fine.

TANIA: Arghhhhhhhh!

PABLO: *(Yelling with her.)* Arghhhhhhh!

   Lights out…a baby cries: Arghhhh!.

Epilogue: Spotlights – One Year and One Month Later

(Maybe we see the gardeners plant the Virginia sweetspire and transform the garden to something beautiful, maybe even magical. Maybe our four protagonists help. Then all actors move to the positions they were in for the Prologue. Maybe someone (Nanny? Gardener?) brings out a baby in a carrier... Maybe the Gomez Gardeners come in.)

PABLO: We decided not to build the six foot one inch fence.

FRANK: I suggested wild rose bushes.

TANIA: Which are beautiful –

VIRGINIA: But they have thorns.

FRANK: So we agreed on a lovely four foot tall Virginia sweetspire

TANIA: A native plant with small green leaves and a tower of white blooms.

PABLO: And planted it right where the property line is supposed to be.

FRANK: I didn't know the fence was in the wrong place.

VIRGINIA: But if we really had looked... we would have seen... that of course the yard wasn't right. We just never noticed. We never needed to notice.

FRANK: The Virginia sweetspire forced me to re-design my garden... I decided to relax and include a couple more indigenous Mid-Atlantic plants. It's a hybrid garden now ... not as formal ...

VIRGINIA: But a lot more interesting! This year Frank won Best Garden.

FRANK: Take that Phillip Saxon!

VIRGINIA: And our new hybrid garden will be the perfect setting for our son's upcoming wedding!

FRANK: To Bill.

TANIA: We trimmed back all the branches on the tree.

FRANK: No acorns getting stuck in my bushes.

VIRGINIA: Less raking. More spiders.

TANIA: Fewer mosquitos! And I planted some peonies.

PABLO: They're so pretty!

TANIA: Some transplants can work well in a native environment.

PABLO: And what better reason to cancel an ill-conceived barbeque than the birth of a baby girl.

TANIA: A girl!

FRANK AND VIRGINIA: A girl!

A beat.

PABLO: Her name is Margarita.

TANIA: Which is 'Daisy' in Spanish

FRANK: A native plant.

VIRGINIA: That is both a weed …

FRANK:… and a flower.

They all look at each other.

VIRGINIA: She is beautiful.

TANIA: I defended my dissertation.

PABLO: And last week, I finally made partner.

TANIA: And I'm expecting again.

VIRGINIA: So soon!!! Irish twins.

FRANK: Sorry– that's an old Polish expression.

VIRGINIA: What?

FRANK: I'm sorry.

PABLO: If I think about it– there's a lot of other ways

VIRGINIA: Very different ways–

FRANK: This little…. episode could have played out.

TANIA: But this is what WE wanted.

Beat. They all look at each other.

TANIA AND PABLO: Old neighborhood

FRANK AND VIRGINIA: New neighbors.

END